SEEING IN THE DARK

SEEING IN THE DARK

A Compendium of Cinemagoing

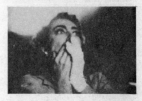

EDITED BY

IAN BREAKWELL

AND PAUL HAMMOND

SERPENT'S
TAIL

Joan Crawford watching herself in Queen Bee

British Library Cataloguing in Publication Data

Seeing in the dark: a compendium of cinema-going

1. Cinema. Films
791.43
ISBN 1-85242-166-2

Library of Congress Catalog Card Number
90-60283

First published 1990 by
Serpent's Tail, 4 Blackstock Mews, London N4

Layout and design by Fiona Keating

Typeset in 10/13pt Medieval Roman by AKM Associates (UK) Ltd

Printed in Great Britain by WBC Print (Bristol) Ltd

SEEING IN THE DARK

IAN BREAKWELL is an artist, video maker, TV performer and diarist. Born in Derbyshire, he lives in London. His most recent books are *Ian Breakwell's Diary 1964–1985* and *The Artist's Dream* (Serpent's Tail, 1988).

PAUL HAMMOND also comes from Derby, and lives in London. He is a painter, author and bookseller. He has written books on Georges Méliès; postcard eroticism; puns (with Patrick Hughes); and cinema and surrealism (*The Shadow and Its Shadow*, 1978; second edition in preparation).

TRAILER

Going to the pictures, the movies, the flicks: *Seeing in the Dark* is about poetic licence in a public place under cover of darkness.

This is where chance comes in. You're in a dreary barn of a place, its halcyon days long gone. You're surrounded by strangers, your dozy curiosity in their sayings and doings dimming as the house lights go down. Then a rectangle of brighter light illuminates the dusty ruched curtains as they glide towards the ceiling. Your neck muscles lock, your body dematerialises. Later, for a whole scene in Fritz Lang's film *You Only Live Once* you find your eyes flitting from a closeup of jailbird Henry Fonda to a dancing hank of fluff stuck in the projector gate. Fonda studiously ignores the hairs as he drawls to an off-screen interrogator. The silhouetted fibres crave his attention. Tension mounts. Finally, the actor's gaze shifts across screen to fix imperiously on the audacious fluff. At that very instant the fluff throws in the towel and sashays from view. The audience stamps and cheers.

It's at moments like this that something magical happens. However engaging the film sequence is in its own right it remains Henry Fonda in a 1930s thriller, a captivating spectre, but a spectre nevertheless. Yet, take an accident like that hair in the gate, put it together with the coincidental gaze of a ghost, and it's as if Fonda really has come back to life. It seems there can never be an absolute spectacle overpowering cowed spectators: some hair will always get in the gate.

We looked almost in vain at one hundred years of literature on cinema for evidence of how going to the pictures is experienced by audiences as a collective rite rich in surreal experience. Film critics and reviewers are obliged to describe films seen either alone, or in the company of fellow professionals, in preview theatres, on video or in archives. Academics study and analyse films in lecture rooms. Yet in public cinemas we, the customers, watch film in the shadowy company of an anonymous crowd, each one of whom, like us, lives a life of which cinemagoing is but a part. Those few studies of cinema audiences that do exist have employed the methods of mass sociology and market research, which cannot fully capture the individual, subjective experience of filmgoing, since they miss out idiosyncratic detail and the personal dreamworld. Measuring applause does not reveal that the movie was memorable for the woman in the third row because the building on screen reminded her of where she went to school and all those childhood memories came flooding back intercut with the film while the auditorium gently shook as an underground train passed beneath and cigarette ash fluttered down from the balcony in the projector beam. And who, sitting in the stalls next to John Hinckley at a matinee of *Taxi Driver*, would have guessed that their neighbour's conclusion from watching the film was that, in order to prove his love for Jodie Foster, he must go out and shoot Ronald Reagan?

So we started by asking our friends, who in turn asked others, until we were eventually inundated with testimonies from witnesses around the world who provided popular proof that there is something about the cinema that encourages, right there in the picture house, thoughts, feelings and behaviour in its patrons by turns enigmatic, terrifying, erotic, sad, hilarious and poetic, often triggered by uncanny interplay between screen image and real-time events in the auditorium and in the world beyond the muffled doors. 'Alone in a crowd' is never so intense as at the movies, and never so open to sudden dislocation. It is the complex play between me, you, them, the film, the cinema building and the world outside that enables us, on occasion, to experience reality more completely, and as in dreams to see in the dark.

IAN BREAKWELL & PAUL HAMMOND

SNOW WHITE

I was three years old. Nobody had told me what a cinema or a film was, and certainly nothing about the concept of an animated cartoon; and I was taken into the largest enclosed space I'd ever seen, into a crowd of strangers, put on a seat, and the lights went out. Figures fifteen feet high loomed over me. The film was *Snow White*; and I felt my sanity slipping until the moment when the queen metamorphosed into the witch. Then I screamed and screamed, and could not stop. My mother called an usherette to have me removed, and I was handed into strange-smelling arms behind a bright beam that dazzled me. The arms hugged my squirming form and carried me out, while my mother stayed to watch the rest of the film. But the exit was at the foot of the screen, and I was being borne up towards that great and drooling hag, away from safety, pinioned by someone I couldn't see, and the witch was laughing.

When we got home I was thrashed for making my mother 'look a fool'. The nightmares began and have haunted me ever since. The witch has my mother's face.

(ALAN GARNER)

SHADOW CAPTURE

There were a few dark places my parents liked to go into besides under their covers in bed. You have to be amazed how young and silly they could be or how solemn with foreboding.

In the midst of summer when you came out, your eyes burned with sunlight and your small meaty smooth arms and legs were stung by the pavement's heat. Or leaving the dark glimmering interior in winter when the ice wind bit through your leggings, mittens and embroidered button holes.

Darkness mysteriously filled with people. Where had they come from? Why had they gathered in the shadowed space? They did not even all know each other, unlike a herd

My mother pinpoints the downfall of western civilisation as the moment when a teenager turned on a transistor radio during a screening of *The Robe*.

(GLEN BAXTER)

We were watching a documentary about Canadian sports. A commentator came on and my mother froze in her seat. 'What's up mum?' I asked. 'That's your father up there on the screen,' she said. It's the only time I ever saw him.

(MURRAY MARTIN)

of cows, a coop of chickens, or a pen of pigs in communal mud.

Two ritual spaces forever commingle. The castle-like stretch to interior sky twinkling with crystal lights. Aroma of incense and in the distance a terrifying version of Santa Claus, haloed in light and shadow as he swung a lamp and chanted hunting sounds. We were immobile on the velvet cushions, my legs sticking out, jacket and skirt velvet enveloped by soft fabric. Nevertheless terror was the measure. That night I began to stutter. My parents often mentioned their remorse, I was speaking so well before we went to the Russian Orthodox Easter Service.

But *Dumbo* was different. We carried sticky ice cream cones into the large dark room. We each had to sit in our own chair. I had crawled into mine and was turning round peering into the dark where many people sat eating popcorn and candy. My parents were pointing up to a beam of light and saying 'Dumbo'. I stared at a huge rectangle of light, it was pinkish floating flickering and suddenly I saw . . . a pig! 'Piglet!' I yelled. 'Piglet!' Piglet was up there! From the book I held on my lap! Piglet who I improved with blue and green crayons was here, huge powerful incandescent unreachable and in motion! I sank into an exquisite passivity staring ahead as dazzling colours flushed and flew, metamorphosing into duck elephant cat dog house. My parents were happy and proud that I was finally seeing what they saw.

(CAROLEE SCHNEEMANN)

TIME FLIES

We were watching Feuillade's *Judex*. Insulated both against the cold and the ordinary activities of the town we abandoned ourselves delightedly, there amidst countless panelled enclosures in this little cinema in the sticks, to the all-consuming comfort of another era. Suddenly on the screen there appears a clock set in the centre of the kind of sumptuous salon that epoch, and Feuillade, alone had a taste for; it shows 4.40 p.m. One of us automatically consults his watch: 4.40 to the second. For an instant our present, across the ruins of several decades, has rejoined that of an afternoon in the 1910s.

(PETR KRAL)

TRAIL

A lone horseman appeared in a vast landscape, a shot rang out in the badlands, dust rose from a wagon train. We crossed the park to get home. My brother walked. I was carried at a smooth lope by Trigger, or sometimes Silver. I sat snug in the tooled leather saddle, the reins lying easily in one hand. Trigger, the palomino, was obedient to the slightest pressure. Thus the magic lasted, and always lasts if the images on the screen take possession.

(JENNI CALDER)

DONKEYS

We drew out of the gravel drive in a perfect crocodile. I was Elizabeth's partner. She wore white ankle socks; my mother preferred me to wear fawn knee-length ones, but our skirts and berets were the same except mine had a leather band inside you couldn't see. Before leaving school we had knelt on the floor in a row to make sure our hem lines touched the ground, just grazed it, and then we had stood up and had our knickers checked. Now we were on the move.

Stage presentation preceding Men of Two Worlds, *London, 1945*

Elizabeth was German and her mother was a clockmaker. I wasn't afraid of Elizabeth but I was frightened of her mother and I was glad the nuns were leading us away from the road where she lived. I didn't like her clockwork elephants.

It was strange seeing nuns outside. I felt ashamed for them.

We were going all the way along Pond Street. We were going to see a film and I hadn't seen a film before.

We followed the nuns to the steps of a tall, gloomy building. We gathered in a long, low room surrounded by pictures of donkeys and men in long striped skirts like shepherds. I was afraid that I was doing something wrong. Being with the nuns only made it feel worse. After being counted one more time, still holding Elizabeth's hand I followed the crocodile miserably through darkened rooms. I wanted to go home.

I was told to sit down and not move. The air was smelly and dim. Elizabeth helped me with the flapping chair. I flattened my thin skirt between my bottom and the furry seat. A silver dish like a holy water font was fastened to the seat in front of me. The bowl was covered in pimples. In the distance a square of light flickered and I heard music swelling. I wrinkled my socks down so they didn't feel so tight, and closed my eyes.

When I woke up Elizabeth was crying, a huge pale donkey was breathing down my neck, and Mother Ignatius was smiling. Her beautiful brown eyes looked at my face. Perhaps she was a donkey too. Everybody sitting around me in the dark knew something that I didn't know, because they were real Catholics and I was only pretending. The film was called *Never Take No For An Answer*, but in my ignorance I didn't even know what the question was. All my friends had been transformed, their faces shone, they couldn't move, while I just rolled my tie up and down and counted the bars on the radiator.

(SELIMA HILL)

When Cinemascope arrived many cinemas 'widened' screens by cropping the picture, thus giving the desired impression. So when old films were shown with projectors masked for 'scope the top of the image, where the most expressive part, the human face, tends to be, was lost. Halfway through *Wuthering Heights* I bitterly complained. Came the reply, 'You're not supposed to see the faces, it's a dark film.'

(RAYMOND DURGNAT)

WORD IS OUT

My mother is holding my hand to stop me getting away across the foyer. I'm looking at the framed portraits of the stars: Anna Neagle, Liz Taylor, Dirk Bogarde, hand coloured like the photographs that Mr Fuller tints, an elderly artist who lives across the road from my grandparents. This is my first visit to the pictures, a treat to take my mind off starting school the following Monday.

'It's the pictures,' I say, pointing.

'Yes. We'll see some *big* pictures in a minute though.'

'Oh'. I know at once that I've made a fool of myself. I remember my father saying earlier that we're going to see a big television. I look around at the milling people, imagining we'll be split up into smaller groups and led through the blank doors to sit in armchairs and watch a TV set on some kind of plinth. I decide to keep my mouth shut about this. We take our seats in the front of the circle and the cinema gradually fills.

A series of ornate gilt mouldings on the walls funnels down towards the brocaded red curtain, arranged into rectangles like the huge old picture frames in Mr Fuller's house, surrounding the dark oil paintings he did as a student and smuggled out of Belgium when he settled here after the Great War. Nowadays he copies postcards,

cropping them to improve the composition. Years later he will show me the sketches he made with mud and chalk in the trenches, of fragile running men and tangled machines, lit up by exploding shells like arrested frames of film.

But for now there are only the empty frames on the walls of the cinema and the rich maroon emulsion they are set against. I wonder if it is here that the pictures are to appear, worrying that the seats are badly arranged, pointing the wrong way, that we won't be able to see them properly. And then the lights go down.

The film is *One Hundred and One Dalmations*. Its images unfold in my mind as effortlessly as a story riding on the voice of a parent, a voice so familiar it disappears, entering in the half-dark, soluble in dreams. My father carries me from the car and I glide up two flights of concrete steps, suspended in midair by anti-gravity. I already know that school is bad news, but behind my lids Miss Fisher and her sidekick, Lavatory-legs Spencer, are receiving diabolical tuition from Cruella De Ville. The school is a locked mansion of empty, high-ceilinged rooms, of dangerous clearings and winding stairs, a country through which children travel in huddled groups of five, flattening them-selves against walls while brave scouts check the route ahead and guard the rear. Word is out. Miss Fisher and her cackling lieutenant are hungry again. I'm new in this place but you've got to learn fast or go under. A girl who's managed to stay alive for a whole year takes me aside and passes on the two basic rules of survival:

1) Never get separated from the others.
2) Always carry a dustpan and brush.

Papillon has just been recaptured for the fourth time. An exasperated Scouser, anxious no doubt to reach The Grapes before half ten, explodes. 'For fuck's sake! Give up, will yer?'

(CHRIS PROCTOR)

The only sure method of avoiding capture, she tells me, is to walk backwards at all times, flicking every particle of dust from every footprint into the dustpan as you go. That way they can't pick up your trail.

(JOHN MUCKLE)

THE BIRD

By the 1960s the Regal had long since had its day. It never drew large crowds and *The Birds* was no exception. During one of the indiscriminate assaults by the murderous flocks of birds the screaming inhabitants of the town ran to and fro in a vain attempt to ward off their attackers. From the cinema itself there also came a piercing cry. The lights were on in a second and the usherette was at the screamer's side. The woman concerned was in a state of shock. A bird had gained entry through one of the broken windows and flown helplessly around until it collided with her. The woman had lashed out in fear and given the bird a fatal blow, feathers everywhere. She was helped from her seat and taken to the rear of the cinema. The remains of the bird were gathered up and removed.

(JOHN WELSON)

THE CHILD'S BRAIN

King Kong plunging to his death from a great height and the real death of a bird in the sky, events dramatic enough for the whirring imagination of a seven year old to cope with.

In the early 1930s part of my childhood was spent at Redcar on Teesside, then as now a down at heel seaside resort surrounded by steel works and wind swept dunes. Yet I hold the town close to my heart, for it is the birthplace of many a dream and memory: it is winter, it was always winter and cold, I am alone on the beach building a secret world, a sand landscape of hills, mountains, ravines with bridges, towns and harbours. Of a sudden a gull which has died on the wing crashes to the sand at my feet, its feathers brushing my forehead as it falls. There it lies, twitching, huge as gulls are huge, and dead, a weird visitor to my private world.

Of the three flea-pits the town boasted my favourite was the Pavilion, at the Coatham end of the prom. It was, in truth, all that remained of what had been the North Pier, blown away by a great storm in the 1920s. Films like dreams come and go and are soon forgotten, yet *King Kong*, which I must have seen in 1933, or early 1934, with its scenes of adventure in a fabled land, was the one to overwhelm my mind and stay with me to the present day. And of those scenes my hero, for that is what Kong had quickly become, tumbling head-over-heels from the roof of the skyscraper to his death on the street was the one to dominate my mind. Death from the sky, again. In my child's brain he crashed at my feet as I walked through a strange city.

(ANTHONY EARNSHAW)

ALFRED: A TRINIDADIAN TALE

The last time I saw Alfred was the day the police shoot them three fellas, remember?

We had just come out of a 12.30 matinee and the street was burning in the sun and those who had come out of the theatre was cool and real but the others in the street were moving in a white light that had them like shadows. Alfred was like us, cool and real, but as the police moved in on him things became a bit confused.

The film had been two of those Kung Fu films. By the time I had gone through the narrow tunnel to pit the first film had already started and I had to use the reflection of the action on the faces of the audience to find a seat without too much of 'Here, Here' and 'Sit down nuh!'. Then the whole 12.30 thing began like it always had since I was small. The whole audience became like one and anything somebody say is like you say it. That afternoon there was a voice among us that seemed to be leading the whole thing — anything he say is what we thinking, but before.

As I saw the circle moving in on Alfred, I realised that that voice had been his. The films were real 'bad' — plenty action and thing — and with Alfred there, our thoughts would gather together and sweep across the screen creating

Many films of my youth were viewed on either side of bouffant and beehive hairdos which filled the centre of the screen. In the hippy era images filtered weakly through a hairy sea of tangled tresses. When afros came in I gave up.

(GEORGE LITTLEBLACK)

Trinidad out of China. At first I thought that was why the police wanted him, because the sort of way we were thinking in there had been definitely subversive, I mean they don't teach you that in school eh! But no. It wasn't that ner. Really, I had heard something about him being involved in some 'group'. After he leave school he had set up some sort of agricultural commune thing, he was always a man like that, saying we were people must make the most of we community skills and thing, but he get squeeze in that farming business and last I hear of him he had gone in the hills and become a guerrilla.

So there he was, all frozen in the hot sun, I began to realise things were really serious when I see them machine guns itching to smoke in the fuzz hand. All of us stand up watching as we come out of the theatre and Alfred glance up at we. Me ain't know what was in that glance, but we moved in behind the police. They shouted for us to stop, but we ain't take that on any more than if they were Chinese in the film, we were recreating our life like how we recreate the film. We were waiting for Alfred to drop he gun, I don't know how we knew he had one but we knew, and slowly he took it out of his waist and dropped it. The police relaxed and move in.

All of a sudden, Alfred strike one karate pose there and leap one leap on the front man, knocking him down, grabbed his machine gun and with two more leaps he was past them and through us as we open up like a black red sea and close again. The police catch theyselves and rush us shouting and some start to shoot, straight into we. That was when they shoot them three fellas, remember, but they ain't get Alfred. He was gone.

(CHRISTOPHER LAIRD)

Written in biro on a scrap of paper stuck on the kiosk window of a cinema in Bangor, Co. Down: 'Closed Due to Lack of People.'
(NOEL SPENCE)

SHORT-SIGHTED DISCIPLE

In Iraq we have 'summer cinema', usually a building next to the real cinema. Because of the heat this second cinema has no roof. The flat roof of our own house was high enough for me to see two summer screens for free. The trouble was they were just too far away to see things clearly, and also I couldn't hear the sound. One day I suggested to my father that he buy me a pair of binoculars. Thus equipped I could watch the films in comfort, switching from one screen to the other. I'd go up there every night and see the same films over and again. One night I saw a film about Jesus Christ. There was a scene in which Christ staggers away from the camera with his cross on his back. I couldn't make out what was going on so I began walking towards the image, binoculars pressed to my eyes. My mother grabbed me at the very edge of the roof, just before I toppled the two storeys to the street.

(SALAH FAIQ)

MISSIONARY

Mosspark Picture House. 1927. Saturday matinee. Age four. A gothic thriller. The tall lantern jawed villain in top hat and tails plays an organ. I am terrified and run home as fast as I can. Years of nightmare. Age thirty-four. I buy a harmonium — nearly an organ — and spend the rest of my life playing it, thickened with doleful dirges, vainly trying to lay the trauma, my only satisfaction the ashen faced, staring eyed audiences staggering out at the end of performances, primed, and ready to carry on the good work.

(IVOR CUTLER)

Now the Bijou, the Globe, the Luxor, the Roxy and the Star are bingo palaces. Old ladies with thick stockings holding veins like knots of worms, and men whose eyes are duller than clay alleys dream other dreams and watch the numbered screen, killing time, hoping for a win. The Empire is a supermarket now, a freezer full of TV dinners where the Gents once stood.

(MIKE HARDING)

MR POWER

There were four of us, and our father, who was the Wesleyan Chapel steward, knew that cinema films would overstimulate our brains, give us over to vain imaginings and, worse, tempt us to worship false gods.

Our mother was an East Riding woman and her regime

was enlightened and less oppressive. Now and then, on Saturday afternoons, she financed a mile and a half walk to Thirsk to visit Power's Picture House. But first we called at Mr Macauley's sweet shop to stock up for the frequent film changes. One of the never mentioned delights of the silent cinema was that you crunched and sucked to your heart's content, annoying nobody but the piano player.

We liked to visit Mr Macauley's shop because his furious brother George played cricket for Yorkshire. You will recall that in 1926, when A W Carr disastrously won the toss and put the Australians in, it was George who bailed us out with an unbeaten 76. You may *not* recall that, when Edgar Oldroyd asked him how he was enjoying a long spell bowling into the wind, he answered, 'It's like bowling up t'bloody cellar steps.'

Although it was a family business I don't think Mr Power worked the projector. Perhaps Mrs Power did. Mr Power can't have done because now and then when rebellion stirred during overlong film repairs he rushed down the aisle cracking a whip. The North Riding is a long way from London. As God is my witness, *he cracked a whip.*

(J L CARR)

GENDER

In 1954 I was eight and every Saturday morning I would set off to the movies with my first boyfriend, ten year old Skippy. For several hours we would be transported via the newsreel to the exotic East, where American soldiers were valiantly fighting the red, or was it yellow peril, and then to the Wild West, where Hoot Gibson or Eddy Dean would be showing cattle rustlers or unfriendly Indians 'what America stood for'. We would spend the afternoon re-enacting in the parking lot behind the apartment what we had seen in the morning on the screen. It was then that I began to discover the fate that awaited me as a female. Whilst I saw myself as the hero's faithful sidekick got up as I was in cowboy gloves with real leather fringes, two guns in holsters buckled on

I introduced Alice Guy's 1913 silent film *A House Divided*. Halfway through the film broke, the houselights came up, and I was accosted by a wino. He insisted that the female lead had worked in Woolworths in Plymouth and he retained an unrequited passion for her. He grabbed me by the throat and began throttling me, all the while demanding her address.

(JUDITH HIGGINBOTTOM)

and tied around the leg for fast draws, ten gallon hat and waistcoat, Skippy insisted that I be the daughter of the murdered rancher whose cattle were being rustled. Gradually it began to dawn on me that while in the celluloid world all things were possible, in the other world it was quite a different story. (Had I been more perceptive I might have noticed that even in the movies women were always the rancher's daughter.)

Years later, on the day our first child was due to be born, when it became obvious that the birth was not imminent, my husband Roger suggested that we go to a film to take our minds off the event. The nearest film was a Canadian thriller called *Shivers*. It turned out to be a story about the residents of a block of flats being used as breeders by aliens, who implant their offspring into the unsuspecting humans. On reaching maturity they begin to wriggle furiously, eventually emerging via the startled human's mouth amid much blood and wailing. Just as the film was reaching its climax my firstborn began one of his frequent exercise periods. So lost was I in the film that for an awful moment I too was about to spawn one of the dreadful aliens.

(MARLENE WINFIELD)

A WOMAN'S PREROGATIVE

Something is troubling the curly-haired boy I'm playing with in the backyard of my grandparents' house. His name is Christopher. We've been prowling around all day on a level with earthworms and rusty, broken down appliances, pressing our ears against the hot wooden trapdoor to the cellar and hearing the silence of ghosts.

'Do you know what The Beatles are?' he asks, letting me climb into his baby pedal car.

'Yes.'

'The Beatles aren't boys, like us. They're men.'

'I know.'

I'm eight and a half years old and disgusted that my mother has to come with me to see *A Hard Day's Night* when usually she just sees me to the edge of the estate and across the main road.

'It's for the kids,' she says to Freda Leader, our next door neighbour. 'Why do they want to go putting an 'A' on with it?' But when she sees the Teds and greasers and hard-faced girls who make up the matinee audience, she thinks it's just as well. We take our seats half way up the stalls. Below us rows of lads have put their winklepickers up on the backs of the seats, their feet crossed at the ankles, perching like a flock of shiny blackbirds with pointed wings.

'All right, missus?' says a boy with a floppy quiff, turning round. My mother's ears are burning and she squirms in her seat. I begin to pronounce the sequence of words and numbers that will prevent her from giving him a piece of her mind.

Then the first film starts. It's called *A Woman's Prerogative*.

'Of course, he didn't understand any of it, so that was all right,' she says later to Freda Leader, in a whisper that echoes around the landing. 'I mean, how could he know what a woman's prerogative is?' She laughs uncertainly. 'I wasn't sure I knew myself.'

That night I lie awake in bed for hours, thinking about this. I remember nothing from the film except a lot of droning talk and a fully clothed woman with dark lashes lying down. What exactly *is* a woman's prerogative? I go through every part of the female body in turn. Bosoms, bottoms, the lot. Suddenly I realise that there must be another part, something like a gap, a hole left by the word I don't understand.

(JOHN MUCKLE)

NATURALISTS

Nineteen fifty two and mother and I were in Bordeaux. My father had excused himself. He had to look after his dahlias. My mother, an innocent at home, aghast when told that 'sod' might mean other than 'earth', was abroad easily befriended by complete strangers. This time they were naturalists. In stature Don Quixote and Sancho Panza.

We drank evening coffee with them. They corrected our accents. The larger one claimed to be minor aristocracy. For the weekend they suggested their camp. 'So much to see, so much to learn'. We caught a late bus out of Bordeaux and arrived in darkness. We were shown our chalet, and then hurried along to the cinema to join the other camp residents. Being shortsighted I moved to the front while my mother stayed at the back. The film was of large happy female peasants dancing, with garlands held aloft. I became aware that my mother was pushing her way towards me. Her face was flushed with excitement. 'The men aren't wearing trousers,' she stage whispered. I looked at her, then behind me. They all had jumpers on but she was right, definitely no trousers.

It is part of the tradition of naturism: no matter how cold you are, off come the pants.

(HILARY PHILLIPS)

CUT FOR CUT

Zaragoza is a windy town. I think that is why it has so many cinema fans and why the best cinema creators in Spain come from there. When I was ten the civil war started. Films were not imported in the fascist zone. Distributors showed repeatedly the old films from their stocks. I must have seen De Mille's *Cleopatra* a dozen times. I used to stay until Claudette Colbert was unrolled from the Persian carpet, then I left.

Cinema was not just an entertainment for our generation. It was a medicine, an antidote to the monstrous reality outdoors. Films reflected another world, where comfort, joy and love were possible. Movies were life and reality, and what happened in the murderous streets an absurd nightmare.

Censorship, dictated by the military and Catholic priests, cut a lot. Dubbing films became obligatory by law, and they

*Doomed cinema, Madrid
(photo: Andrew Greaves,
1985)*

took advantage of it to change the dialogue. In their anxiety
to eliminate sinful love they presented lovers as relatives,
thus transforming the boring Hollywood sex code into a
frolic of perversions. We could see Garbo kissing her father
in a most peculiar way, and Ava Gardner seducing her
brother, Clark Gable, in *Mogambo*.

At sixteen I discovered an old man who exhibited silent
films in villages. He rented me a projector, and because he
wanted to retire sold his movies to me for a few pesetas a
twelve-reeler. Some of the classics were in excellent
condition, as he had seldom showed them. They later
became part of the collection of the National Film Library.
But most of the material was falling to pieces. I had to learn
to cut off the rotten celluloid and splice together the usable
bits. When projecting the resulting film the jump cuts of
the narrative could produce interesting surprises. Soon I
mixed in bits of different movies: Lady Windermere
looking down from her balcony and seeing . . . whatever!
Most of my splicing I did at random, automatically. When I
had completed a two hour programme my friends came to
my home and we saw it together. The Buñuel family was
particularly fond of these programmes. And that was the
start of the first film society in Spain during the Franco
dictatorship.

(J F ARANDA)

GOLD RUSH RUE EVERLOR

The war was over. The family were staying with a friend of my grandmother's in La Ciotat, a small harbour town near Marseille, our normal home. I remember a dark apartment, ships' masts, a smell of tar, iron and iodine, grownups. My father said, '*Je vais t'emmener au cinéma ce soir voir* La Ruée vers l'or.' 'I am going to take you to the pictures tonight to see *The Gold Rush*.' I did not know what 'cinéma' was, it was one of those wonderful and unimaginable pleasures like *La Semaine de Suzette* and its doll Bleuette, which the war had taken away. Grown-ups would evoke them discreetly, so as not to make you envious, not to corrupt you with impossible desires. They would say, '*Avant guerre, tu vois, il y avait …*' 'Before the war, there was …' My grandmother had a beautiful satin box with flowers painted on the cover. She hoarded ribbons in it. She said, 'You see, before the war, this was given to me as a present, and it was full of chocolates.' I could not imagine what they were, apart from an unattainable marvel, part of a world gone for ever. I thought that the ribbons were beautiful, all the colours of the bunch of flowers painted on the cover.

Now all these things were returning, one by one. Cinema was one of them.

We went late one evening. I remember dark streets, and walking hand in hand with my father. I had misunderstood the name of the film, and not dared ask too many questions. You were supposed to be bright if you took things in quickly. I liked to play at being bright. I had vaguely understood something about a press of people, and was surprised to see the streets so empty. I had heard, not *La Ruée vers l'or*, '*ruée*' being quite outside the bounds of my vocabulary, but '*La rue Everlor*'. Everlord, Everlaure, Héverlore, Aiverlaur? It would be foreign, magical. Each of the streets through which we went might have led to it. I remember I kept saying, 'Is this it?' and my father said, 'No, a bit further.' I loved my father, and he loved me. It was so intense and we were both so strung up, uneasy about it. But exalted. All this spare passion between us, which we did not know how to show. So we were exceedingly well-behaved towards each other. I was promising myself to be very quiet, whatever it would be. He was coaxing me to walk a bit further without having to carry me, by promising that it was just a bit further. It was all part of the Rue Everlor.

When he did say *'nous voilà!'* I just didn't get it. It was a house, a kind of shop with a rather dingy entrance. People were queueing to get in, but without ration stamps.

I never twigged what the gold rush was. It took me years to finally comprehend. But the house hanging over the cliff got me into agonies of suspense, and I was amazed, when the dark came without bombs, by how the black on the screen, especially the black of Charlie Chaplin's suit, his moustache, hat and rolling intense eyes, fitted the darkness of the little cinema. And how the white, the snow, the sheet that was the screen, *was* the light, and you forgot yourself when you were watching. The hunger that made Charlie, Charlot, chew the boiled slices of boot, moustache toing and froing under his nose, I understood as well or as little as the hunger of the grown-ups around me, my mother eating the woodworms along with the oats and the silence as everybody stopped to watch her. I was lucky, thin as a rail and never hungry.

I remember the terror though: when the bear comes out of the wood and stalks after unsuspecting Charlot on the steep, cliff-edged mountain path. I remember screaming and my scream breaking into ecstatic laughter and relief as the bear, instead of eating Charlot, started walking splay-footed in imitation of him, then went back into the wood. Yes, the war was over. And Charlot never even noticed.

(NICOLE WARD JOUVE)

WAR GAMES

Now aged seventy-four I have lived the past fifty years within hailing distance of Earl Grey's monument: he of the 1832 Reform Act. Towering over the modern centre of Newcastle, the provincial capital of the north east, and facing Tyne-wards, he surveys the ancient city. I was born

Nothing will ever feel as real as those times. No other world will take me so fully into its secret ways. No oranges will taste the same as those we ate on those Saturday mornings, saving the peel to throw at the screen when Roy Rogers brought out his guitar to serenade Dale Evans across a Texas campfire that was flickering in an enchanted cave in a Manchester street.

(MIKE HARDING)

into the war torn world of May 1915 in a mile long street of
two storey houses strategically located between Wallsend
railway station and Wallsend drill hall. It was the kind of
street that money-grabbing, rather than socially inspired,
landlords provided, and thus created their lasting and
unenviable reputation. No bathroom, no indoor water and
an outside ash closet. The back lane could have provided
the set for Chaplin's *The Kid*. The wartime government had
promised the troops they would return to 'homes fit for
heroes to live in', but the sick joke was that you had to be a
hero to survive in them. I remember black faced miners and
not so black faced shipyard workers passing to and fro to
the nearby yards or the 'G' pit at the end of the street. Much
more inspiring and less frequent were the sight and sounds
of soldiers marching to war from drill hall to station. Less
inspiring was the sight of those returning. By 1919 the
number of soldiers began to decrease and the numbers of
unemployed to increase. My father was one of them, and
when 'Buddy Can You Spare a Dime?' topped what was then
the hit parade, its lyrics summed up the poverty, de-
pendence and despair of the millions of poor throughout
the world. We all knew how little and how vital a dime was.
A few ex-soldiers volunteered for the White Army, an
unsuccessful venture designed to strangle the Russian
Revolution at birth. But most of them stood on street
corners.

On first seeing *All Quiet on the Western Front* it was as
if the whole cast had marched through my life on their way
to Wallsend station and the battlefields of Europe. With a
little imagination I envisaged the hopes and fears, and the
overwhelming horrors these young men had to face. When
Lew Ayres reached out to that ephemeral alighted butterfly
his expression revealed the most delicately sensitive
emotion I had experienced until then. In a flash a sniper,
who could have been any gun happy soul anywhere, had
killed. That contrast of tender sensibility and senseless
brutality was etched into my mind, exposing the utter
meaninglessness of violence and war.

By the time I was ten it seemed I had lived backstage to
so many of those early film sets. It was the revolutionaries
who were the villains, the Royals and their supporters the

good and kind and handsome heroes. *Their* enemies were villains with downturned mouth and black moustache, not then Russian, always French. The crowds that lined the roads on the way to the guillotine looked much like most of the people in Wallsend. And the women seemed to knit the same kind of loops my mother did. The next street towards the River Tyne was under the railway arch. Hadrian Road was named after the Roman emperor who, we agreed, must have genetically bequeathed to us some superlative qualities. What more natural then that we could hang up our football boots, change into our French cavaliers' outfits or as quickly become Roman gladiators? Ben Hur's chariot race was re-enacted around the Roman Wall, too neatly preserved in Wallsend Park. With iron gords, or hoops as the rich people called them, and with clashes and tensions no less thrilling and dangerous than the real thing, we competitively raced until we dropped. Then our ash closets were exchanged for flush toilets. The new metal dustbins were quickly lidless. Armed with wooden swords, cardboard breast plates, and now shields, we set off with renewed enthusiasm. Hand to hand fighting dominated our imagination as if right and wrong, good and bad, had to be decided in violent confrontation on the spot or at some predetermined location. And the reward, as our film heroes had it, was the beautiful lady. Alas, we always had to return to our cobbled back lanes. If, as frequently happened, two of us would fall out and come to blows, then passers-by would stop, form a circle and watch without intervening, confirming their view that justice would be achieved this way.

As I took my place with two jamjars in my first Saturday morning kids matinee queue, apprehensive lest the currency had been devalued or even replaced with money, I observed that not only were Royals the heroes in the films but that my choice of cinema was between the Queens and the Royal, and I was warned that before the performance you were supposed to stand for the pianist's rendition of 'God Save the King'. I took against this practice and reflected later that 'God Save the People of Wallsend' would have been more appropriate, for few in authority cared much, let alone had the power to assuage the people's

Foyer display with live bat, London, 1960

meagre needs.

Then we moved into a street called Portugal Place. Not even the most persuasive estate agent could have produced one environmental reason for moving there; but it was a miner's house and rent free. Certainly my mother's success-ful campaign to have the nearby men's urinal closed was vigorous and rewarding. The town's mortuary adjoined the urinal. At that time it would provide a resting place for six to ten clients a week, and the arrival of each one had the macabre side of me guessing what kind of corpse it was. On odd nights that would worry me but in time I realised they were the kind of neighbours who never caused a disturbance.

But there was a third amenity, and vitally essential it was: the corporation depot, with its stables and Clydesdale horses and endless line of carts. Horse manure, horse muck or just plain horse shit, depending on your susceptibilities, was a much needed and highly effective fertiliser for the allotments, and so from an early age a daily chore was to keep an eye open for droppings, grab your shovel and bucket and run out to scoop it up. Portugal Place was to the supply of horse shit what Wimbledon 'insiders' are to Centre Court tickets on final days. You could almost stand and wait for a horse to deliver.

I want you to recall with me Chaplin in *City Lights*. Charlie has taken a street sweeper's job to earn the money to pay off the cruel landlord who would otherwise put a blind girl and her mother out onto the streets. It was like that in Wallsend in those days. In addition Charlie needs to raise enough money to finance an operation to restore the girl's sight. No money, no sight: the way it was before the National Health Service came to Wallsend. Imagine Charlie with his sweeping brush and shovel neatly disposing of a pile of horse droppings and then, looking into the camera, observing a passing elephant. A twitch of his moustache, a movement of the eyebrow, and what else did he need to do? When the new sighted flower girl sees not a handsome, well groomed, six foot Adonis her eyes reveal something different. You see *he was a hero*, a social hero, a small guy, a fall guy, not necessarily a brave or courageous guy, usually the opposite. Chaplin was telling me that such people don't qualify for medals or monuments, unlike those who fight and kill or wound, or are killed or wounded. I was and remain a supporter of Chaplin's view.

(T DAN SMITH)

SEARCH LIGHT FOR QUALITY

'Rotting Hill! Shocking Hill!' was the 52 bus conductor's cabaret turn on his every approach to Notting Hill. And so it was with the Notting Hill Gate Classic cinema around 1969. At one late-night show the main picture was projected in the reel order 1, 2, 5, 4, 6, 3, 7. The line I took with the manager was that, as a composer of music for films, I really needed to see equal commitment all along the picture beam to the public. 'I don't see any other dissatisfied customers' was his reply. This cinema had also capitalised on the psycho-acoustic phenomenon prevalent in rock music of suggesting heightened intensity with 'fuzz': the speaker cone had plainly blown, rendering all dialogue and music as if through comb and paper. And the projector's arc lamps were not so much set as sunset, through a fog. How poignantly vignetted was the ice in *Alexander Nevsky*, but Eisenstein would have stabbed the projectionist with icicles.

(RON GEESIN)

I saw tombs open and the terrifying silhouettes of walking corpses set out on the road. That night I couldn't close my eyes, the slightest creaking of the furniture announcing the imminent arrival of the undead. My screams of terror awoke my parents and brought them rushing in panic to my room.

(NELLY KAPLAN)

ANTHEM

When we attended film shows in the RAF the National Anthem was played *before* the picture, accompanied by film footage of the Queen riding side saddle down Horse Guards Parade. We had wagers on how many times the horse's prick bounced back and forth in the time it took to cross the Parade. Arguments were fierce: some said six, some six and a half, some seven. As we all stood to

You left the cinema your hand in your pocket clutching a non-existent 'rod', you went rat a tat tat Chicago piano machine gun style and did a James Cagney hoodlum staggering along the pavement with your hands to your chest until you collapsed into a doorway mown down by gangsters' bullets crying for Pat O'Brien or Joan Blondell to take the message to ma. It was a great way to die.
(ARTHUR MOYSE)

attention in the darkened cinema, singing the anthem, we would count them off: 'God save our — one — gracious Queen — two — Long live our — three — noble Queen — four.'

(ALF MACGABHAN)

WITNESSES

Try watching *Witness* in Dublin, where the inhabitants use films as an aid to conversation. Every appearance of the boy Samuel is greeted with, 'Ah, doesn't he just remind you of Kevin/Michael/little Christy? Sure, they're all coming up on the bus from Mullingar/Limerick/Cork on Friday for the whole weekend.' Even when Samuel is facing death by having his throat cut in the Gents the exchange goes like this, 'Mother of Mary, that reminds me of my poor Joseph going. Didn't he have the anaemia, and the Hodgkiss, and a touch of leukaemia too. How's your own then?'

(ROGER WAKELING)

BEST OF BRITISH

The Odd Hour Cinema, Nottingham, the 1950s. You went in, you came out; whenever you felt like it. Through a tiny door off the dry page of the street, from the cold light of day to sitting in womb-like blackness. Where did the giant images come from? I didn't know. I knew only that they happened there in the darkness and only a few feet from the pavements. The blackness enveloped so warm and close and, I believed, extended infinitely away from the street on all sides, something that made any street plan impossible. And I believed that this world of darkness and changing images went on without a break, as unceasingly as the other less real one outside, wherever outside was, and by some unlikely philanthropic gesture of the city corporation was allowed to co-exist and be connected by the little dark doors with dark portholes. In the darkness I felt in the hands of God, someone who could do anything He liked with me, even though that someone was more likely to be Mr Slieman, the manager, who with his pencil moustache looked more like a used car salesman and was constantly trying to show Louise, the cashier and kiosk girl, his collection of prophylactics.

The Dale cinema. Early 1960s. A time of endless summer evenings, Bobby Rydell and Bobby Vee. The last drainpiped leg of the Teddy boy era. And the last show at this austere palace in the area of Nottingham full of smoke and even less substantial youthful dreams. The one would be abolished by the Clean Air Act and the others would die and disappear one by one, passing through the gates of the fatal factories close by. The final curtain as it was for so many cinemas at this time, before they became cash and carry warehouses for bowls and colanders, brushes, clothes pegs, cloths and uncountable tons of things being produced in orange plastic. After that they slipped into anonymity, disappearing altogether into the buildings surrounding them, turning into workshops for alloy welding and serious industrial accidents.

The Dale, perhaps for the only time in its short life, was full. The word 'anticipatory' falls limply from its first syllable in its attempt to describe the atmosphere, re-charged from row to row. Young next to old, doing-well next to down-and-out: a heterogeneous mass present for its own mutually exclusive reasons. The buzz, the unin-hibited, excited talking, yes, uninhibited talking, in a district where you were made to feel peculiar if you allowed any expression to cross your face in the street, died as the lights slowly faded. Complete darkness. Then, in that second of hushed silence before the screen and fanfare blaze out, there came from the middle of the auditorium a huge and shocked voice 'What the fookin' 'ell are yo' doin'?', followed almost at once by two mighty smacks that could only have been someone being hit. The fanfare seized up on its first chord and then seemed to fall over itself, collapsing in a welter of notes. The first frame of the programme appeared for a moment, juddered, then disappeared. The

It was a low-down dirty day. I was leading the life of a bat in a dark hole, eating candy and gobbling images. I plugged my naked feet in between the empty seats as tears rolled down my cheeks. I've learned to cry silently during movies.

(LYNNE TILLMAN)

Halfway through *Hush, Hush, Sweet Charlotte* big white subtitles came up saying YOUR MOTHER IS GOING TO DIE. For weeks afterwards I prayed for her, though I'm not religious and she seemed as fit as ever. Then one day my father sat me down and said, 'Lisa, I have some bad news I'm afraid.' I interrupted him and said, 'It's about mother isn't it? I know already. I went to see a film last month and the film told me.'

(LISA MONTAGUE)

lights came up and we were not in that magic world beyond the screen but back in the familiar tawdry surroundings of Sneinton, Notts. A gargantuan Teddy boy was standing in the stalls, looking down at his feet. The seat next to him was now empty. The torches, that had from the back played on and around him like searchlights finding the enemy, were switched off. Disbelief vied with sideboards as extensive and useless as Chesil Bank for domination of his face. He looked up and all the way round; all eyes were on him. He pointed down under the seats: the edge of a shabby raincoat could just be seen. In a voice full of virginal astonishment he said, ' 'E were touchin' me fookin' cock.' A B western hero hiding up a gully while the posse rush blindly past was believable. This was not. The police arrived, three stripes followed by a constable. There was some cheering. It was a great performance by the sergeant as he strolled up to The Mighty Tharg. The PC seemed a trifle unnerved playing to a full house. The sergeant spoke inaudibly to the Ted and they began to escort him out, one on each side. Halfway up the aisle the Ted turned his head again to the packed house and in the same pained voice of injured innocence repeated, ' 'E were touchin' me fookin' cock.'

The Scala in the 1960s showed all-night horror films. There were as usual only a few lone silent figures, sitting in isolation. One, after watching the first two films, was hunched at the end of a row, asleep and snoring. Except this time there was another, a thin, raincoated, restless figure. I watched his silhouette moving from seat to seat, watching the others, shuffling and sidling closer, sometimes stopping as if uncertain, but then moving again until he was next to someone. Then he'd sit for a while, occasionally glancing at the figure next to him, until at last he'd lean towards the other's ear. The response was to push him off or to move away or no response at all. Then the silhouette looked round again and began to move towards someone else. An all-nighter was a triumph of will and my eyelids were already dropping, but I kept my eyes on the thin figure. He would get to me soon. Though the film was running I had seen no staff in the cinema for hours. The film, *Mr Sardonicus*, was about a man whose face has frozen into a wide and terrible corpse-like grin. The silhouette sat down next to the snoring man, and looked hard at him. I felt uneasy. The thin figure leaned over and whispered in the sleeper's ear. The man screamed, fell off his seat, and rolled down the aisle to the front. He was awake by then, as was everyone else. The thin figure had slipped through the velvet curtains and was away.

The Odeon, St Albans, the 1970s. The film *Shivers*, a real horror of bloody worm-like parasites the size of Errol Flynn's penis. In front of me five youths, age seventeen, leaning back, arms spread, cool, sniggering and making jokes, pretending not to be frightened. Next to me a girl eating a box of liquorice torpedoes. On the screen a woman nonchalantly opens the lid of a washing machine and out leaps one of the Things. Everyone in the cinema, everyone except the five youths, jumps and screams. The box of liquorice torpedoes leaves the hand of the girl next to me. As if in a slow motion sequence from a Peckinpah film I see the torpedoes escape from the box, turn head over tail as they rise, reach their zenith, and begin falling again, towards the heads and shoulders of the youths in front. The sweets land. The youths jump up, shouting with terror and disgust and begin waving their arms about, flapping at the air, furiously brushing their hair and shirts. Jumping up they have made everyone else jump again. Then they see the torpedoes. They laugh now, but are shaking with the release of tension. Everyone laughs, not at them but with them. The youths are still standing, trembling, laughing. They meet the eyes of others. They admit their fear. Everyone is shivering together. It is a lovely moment.

A little place on the Tottenham Court Road. The 1980s. The sort of place that still does double features, which it was doing that bright sunny afternoon. My wife and I went up to the pay booth. A friendly Asian face looked through at us, gave us our tickets, and pointed to the black double doors further in. We paused at the kiosk. The face disappeared from the pay booth and appeared again in front of us and sold us a packet of sweets. We went on towards the double doors. The friendly little Asian appeared from another door and held his hands out for our tickets. He tore them, passed half back to us, pointed to the doors again and

said, 'Anywhere you like.' I opened the black doors and we entered. From behind the screen curtains an organ played a jolly tune. There was no one else in the cinema. It seemed so sad I could have cried. We sat down. After a minute or two the Asian suddenly slid out from the side of the big curtains and then stopped, a tray of drinks and ice creams round his neck. He just stood there, right at the front with the curtains at his back, staring into the auditorium. We stared back; there was nowhere else to look. I had to walk down and buy something, lots of things. He smiled and said 'Thank you' as if he'd never seen me before, as did I. I went back to my seat and faced the front again. He stayed there a little longer, then disappeared back into the curtains. The organ went on playing. I wondered if it was him, playing on a pre-recorded tape; or his brother. Whose face would it be, looking through the small square window behind us? The films started and finished on time. He was there at the end, opening the double doors for us. We went out into the bright sunny street. The traffic and the crowds were passing interminably in each direction, as they had been all the time.

If the cinema is right the film need hardly matter. Mr Slieman may still be spending most of his working day shuffling ever closer to Louise, unaware or uninterested in the magic he and his house create. But it is still there: the soaring vague walls and giant secretive curtain washed with colours you've only dreamt about, the colour of all the things you were never allowed to have as a child, suddenly real and there before you.

(ROGER WAKELING)

THE PERSIAN PANTHEON

Siah Armanjani once told me how he used to see the movies in his native Persia in the 1950s. He said there was a person, famous throughout the land, whose job it was to visit the halls where films were being shown and to describe the films to the local people. This man provided a

During a scene in W C Fields' *The Bank Dick* in which men were digging a trench in the road I became aware that my feet felt cold and wet. Looking down I saw they were in a puddle of water that hadn't been there at the start and seemed to be oozing out of the ground.

(IAN BREAKWELL)

running commentary on the events on the screen, which were otherwise a fabulous mystery. His non-stop verbal explications, declaimed as he strode up and down the crowded aisles, described the gods and mythology and history of the people of Persia; and his improvisation fitted what was happening in the film as the hair fits the head. In this way were seen *Gone With the Wind* and *All Quiet on the Western Front*: as events in the nation's history, peopled by characters from the Persian pantheon. At the same time, our poet's impromptu verses — often he hadn't seen the film before — were in the complex scheme of Persian poetry, rhyming, scanning, and so on. Armanjani reported to me that at the height of his powers our man sometimes accompanied a two hour programme of film trailers spliced together. The popular poet's imagination, skill and learning could concoct, at that instant, a sustained story with a cast of hundreds that linked all those wars, love affairs, catastrophes, comedies and come-what-may into a coherent whole.

Since Siah told me this story about a supreme storyteller, I have told the story myself many times. I think it has grown in the telling.

(PATRICK HUGHES)

GUN LORE

As a child I was given a grey plastic gun as a birthday present. Working on the torch principle the gun became a simple projector. Hinged along its top edge, it was possible to open the gun so that a film loop could be inserted round its profile. Two small batteries fitted the butt while the beam escaped at the muzzle. One of my greatest pleasures was to load my gun, draw the curtains in my bedroom and then crawl under the bed. I was now completely in the dark and it was here that I would shoot whatever film I had onto the skirting board of my makeshift cinema.

(LES COLEMAN)

BEING

I was the bad gunslinger who was new in town, and the snot-faced boy who wore army boots but no socks was the good cowboy. As agreed, he swung a punch to my chin so that I should rise in an elegant arc of slow motion to fall sprawled in a dramatic contortion on the bar room floor. I fell hard against the asphalt playground and I felt the pain that had not been visible on film.

When my brother looked through his new spectacles into the Cinemascope format of the wide mirror I saw that he gently let his lower jaw fall a little so as to give himself more of the thin-faced appearance of Hank B Marvin in *Summer Holiday*. Once, when he was the centre of attention at the youth club I saw him do it again. The other people seemed not to notice. They were all being in other films.

(TIMOTHY EMLYN JONES)

ESSOLDO AND ENVIRONS

For me, movies and play were enmeshed during childhood, a certain cinema and its environs being both stimulus and setting for my juvenile adventures to the extent that, thirty years later, its contours and hidey holes still haunt my dreams.

At the height of the Teddy boy era the local cinema foolishly premiered *Rock Around the Clock* on Bonfire Night. Bangers punctuated the soundtrack, snow fountains cascaded in the aisles, and the film ended abruptly when a five-bob rocket went straight through Bill Haley's open mouth.

(GEORGE LITTLEBLACK)

When not submitting to its weekly invasion by hordes of kids, the back and sides of the Deco-fronted Essoldo in Chaddesden bore silent witness to our after-school games. This monolith sat atop an escarpment which accommodated the raking of the auditorium and the levelled hardcore of a car park, and cast its long shadow over an adjacent bit of parkland, a cosy corner of scrub, stream and wood that drew me and my friends to it like a magnet. We rarely played close to the building which, when not lit up, had something of the baleful haunted house about it. And the car park was too rutted and stony to permit ball games, far too exposed to sustain our hiding and seeking, tick and

nicking. This car park was not without charm, however. In wet weather it was a site for spectacular puddles, a mucky moat from which the picture house rose like a medieval castle. In one corner of the lot was a sad, wet-rotten arch which bore the legend 'For Patrons Only'. Just what was a 'patron' I wondered? In another corner was an equally decrepit cabinet which displayed a handful of publicity stills that were changed twice weekly, along with the dayglo signwriting on the marquee, as if by legerdemain. One day we were poking around in some sodden ashes by the rear exit and found a few slivers of celluloid with images on them. In trying to conceal his negligence the projectionist had provided me with tangible evidence of the grand illusion. I couldn't be sure how, but felt that a truth had been revealed.

Come five o'clock on a Saturday afternoon you'd bundle your way out of the pictures, delirious with image overload, to be hit between the eyes by the blinding light of day and a balmy blanket of heat. You'd hesitate to drink in the hallucinatory detail of the visual field, to assimilate the odd distancing of natural sound, before joyously plunging with your cronies into your outdoor make-believe. The park was reached via a slippery slope. As we slid at speed down the escarpment we took care to avoid nettles and barbed wire, then we'd squeeze between the splintery struts of the Essoldo's picket fence. Once through, we really cut loose. This bit of park had just enough hint of wilderness to be readily transformed in imagination into prairie, canyon, rain forest, river delta, open sea. Our hinterland of the imaginary actually consisted of grass tussocks, brambles, a grove of willows, some hawthorns, a beech tree or two, drainage ditches, a slow and deep brook with steep banks, a weir, twin tunnels which took the stream beneath the main Derby to Nottingham road and, upstream, a wooden footbridge and wobbly stepping stones. All in all, the perfect showcase for a new identity as hero. I recall imitating a stunt performed by the obscure Buffalo Bill Jnr in a Poverty Row serial, when he outwitted his pursuers by swinging at speed from saddle into tree. On dry summer days the dust raised by galloping posses could be evoked by a vigorous soft shoe shuffle in the red Derbyshire clay, your sandals given spurs by a twig slid in by the outer ankle. Any film appearance by Robin Hood reinforced a belief that this wooded playground was surely once part of a Sherwood Forest. Our village had been written into the Domesday Book. The park itself, only an arrow's flight from the movie theatre, still had the undulations of a feudal field system. And the ecclesiastical yew wood slightly further afield would, we convinced ourselves, have been a perfect provider of the English yeoman's longbow.

The muscular derring-do of our film heroes inspired us to imitative feats of climbing, usually trees; and their prowess in stalking and sniffing out was echoed in our exploration of sombre, dingy and often damp places. Up into the light, down into the dark. The willows between Essoldo and stream were old, stunted and easy to climb. Some were split and bent almost double by their own mass, which meant you could charge straight up them into the lower branches six feet above ground. All were hollow, and with care, for there were protruding knots to buffet and bruise you, you could lower yourself into their embrace and experience the exquisite anxiety of claustrophobia and entrapment. Looking up you would see an alluring smidgen of sky through the spiky branches. The stream, tumbling over the weir, spread itself and then disappeared into two tunnels. (The 'For Patrons Only' sign loomed over this pool.) One of these tunnels, which seemed awesomely long, black and terrifying, was, with gumption and at such times as the brook was not in full spate, explorable. When at last your gum boots got you, bent double, to the other end you could straighten up to see, again framed in foliage, the mature dream gardens of well-off homeowners, their sumptuous spreads a far cry from the fresh plots of intractable clay that fronted our council houses. Somewhere a big old penny dropped. Why of course: the Essoldo had been built for these middle class folk in the 1930s — *they* were Patrons!

(PAUL HAMMOND)

Dear Son,
There is a shilling on the mantelpiece. Do not see any X films. Get yourself a bag of chips on the way home.

(MRS FINCH)

A HOLE IN THE SCREEN

In the 1940s we lived alongside a cinema, in a small town lost in the southern pampas of Argentina. The cinema was immediately adjacent to our house, so that every night we could hear the film and imagine what was on the screen. All of us that is except uncle Eugenio, who had never been to see a film, saying that it was a fraud, all illusion, and that when the lights went up and all the characters disappeared the screen was no more than a rag. When he saw us coming back from the movies every Sunday, discussing the film, he would say, 'I don't believe it. I never would have credited that people would talk about these illusions as if they'd really taken place.' He regarded us as stupid and ignorant. If the film had a sad ending aunt Delicia, who always took anybody's love affair for her own, would return home crying. 'Poor thing,' she'd sob, thinking about the heroine, and she'd get undressed so that she could carry on crying in bed. Uncle Eugenio would get mad with frustration, utterly unable to find the words to refute the fact that illusions might provoke real tears.

We convinced him in Holy Week. They were showing a film, *The Life of Christ*, and though this was clearly an illusion as well it had taken place in real life, and uncle was very much a believer. He went in acting very worried, looking at people as though ashamed that they were seeing him in a cinema. But five minutes into the film he was as possessed as when he was down at the football stadium watching a match.

When uncle Eugenio saw Judas striking a bargain with the Romans he cried out 'I can't stand this!' and ran out of the movie theatre. He reappeared with his shotgun just at the moment Judas was handing over his master. And so as not to hurt anyone inadvertently uncle Eugenio waited until the apostle was some way from the rest of the crowd.

The hole in the screen coincided with screams and the lights going up and the immediate disappearance of the images. In the midst of the smell and dust of his incredible deed, and the smoke from the gunshot, it was uncle Eugenio who seemed like an illusion.

(DANIEL MOYANO)

To humour me my patient father agrees yet again to my choice of film. He has endured most of the French New Wave, and anyway is content if the seats are comfortable and conducive to naps. This evening my choice is *Last Year at Marienbad*. During one of the long corridor scenes dad falls asleep. He wakes up much later during another corridor scene. 'Mmm,' he remarks, 'that was a long corridor.'

(PETE AYRTON)

HOLY SMOKE

Twice I was at the cinema when it burned down. The first to go was the Alamein. Panic ensued. Fathers deserted their children. The cowboy film carried on playing. When we got out there were hundreds watching the blaze. This was Allah's revenge, they said. The second was the Gazi. The fire started in the projection box. From inside we could hear screams of 'Please, open the door!' Then the exits burst open and we swarmed out. Again there was an assembled audience for the conflagration. Because a mosque stood next door it was said that the cinema had been rejected by Allah as an unworthy neighbour. Rumour had it the owner of the Gazi burned it down for the insurance money. A bank was built on the site, a much better class of neighbour for the place of prayer.

(SALAH FAIQ)

PROTESTORS FAIL AS FILM IS SHOWN

Strident protests and strict security checks on everyone entering the Cork Opera House seriously delayed the screening of *The Last Temptation of Christ* as part of Cork Film Festival last night.

The first public showing of what many Catholics view as Martin Scorsese's outrageous interpretation of the Biblical epic drew both predictable and highly unpredictable howls.

The advice of Bishop Michael Murphy to his flock to stay away was heeded. The great bulk of those who thronged Emmett Place last night wanted to see the film, and they outnumbered protestors by a minimum of ten to one.

Extra security was designed to prevent trouble inside the Opera House. One man was evicted when he was discovered to be carrying two small cans of paint.

What was unpredictable about the protest was a devastatingly subversive counter protest by a small group who said they were present 'on behalf of the acolytes of Our

Lady of Ballinspittle' and who said they wanted to 'protect the rights of blasphemers and heretics and Nobel prize-winning great novelists'.

As the small group of less than one hundred people genuinely opposed to the showing of the film sang hymns and said the rosary, the group of luridly dressed and made up 'acolytes' loudly parodied their prayers with phrases like 'General Franco, pray for us' and 'General Pinochet, stand by us'.

Those anti the showing declined to give their names and said they had come as individuals. Those anti the pro-testors declined to give their names and said they were there as individuals.

The protestors carried placards saying things like: 'Jesus, in Him there is no sin', 'It's a sin to go in' and 'It is the work of the devil'. Those protesting against the protestors had placards stating 'Mary Mag was a Hag' and 'Jesus was nailed not screwed.'

When the lone girl 'acolyte' had the word 'screwed' torn off her placard by an exasperated protestor she said. 'My fellow Christians are welcome to my placard, all they have to do is ask.'

A protester against the showing of The Last Temptation of Christ *tears a placard carried by an acolyte of Our Lady of Ballinspittle outside Cork Opera House (photo: Des Barry, 1988)*

41

The illuminated Moorish fountain in the cinema foyer contained goldfish. One day a cable shorted and they were electrocuted. But not killed: instead it put a uniform kink in their spines. Afterwards the fish swam in jerky circles.

(PAUL HAMMOND)

The genuine protestors were mostly middle aged and assembled outside the Opera House from 7 p.m. One group of sixteen came from Ballyvourney by bus, another smaller group came from Ballinspittle and there were more from the city. There were no clerics nor foreigners amongst them and it was obvious that many of those going in to view the film viewed them as a sad little group.

One man said it was significant that this was the 33rd Cork Film Festival and Christ died when he was thirty-three. 'Maybe the Film Festival will die at thirty-three as well. I hope it does,' he said.

Opponents of the film carried pamphlets which they distributed. These stated: 'Everybody who calls himself or herself a Christian must now rally to the side of Christ and defend Him, not only with their rosaries and prayers but by protesting in a public and persistent manner against this film.'

This stern injunction was widely ignored in Cork last night.

(DES O'SULLIVAN, *The Cork Examiner*, 4.10.88)

DARBY O'GILL AND THE LITTLE PEOPLE

I saw heretics beheaded, martyrs burned at the stake, Mexicans massacred, gooks machine gunned, Indians annihilated; and strolled home happy. But when the death coach came galloping out of the wild black sky to take Darby O'Gill to hell, it fairly put the fear of God in me; more so than any clergyman before or since, however vivid their threats of eternal damnation.

The Sunday sermon was so predictable, as were the plots and stock characters in every cowboy, pirate or war film. In those early pre-TV Saturday afternoon matinee days at the Ideal cinema in Carrickfergus, only two movies broke the mould for me and lodged themselves forever in the imagination: *The Wizard of Oz* and *Darby O'Gill and the Little People*. Kansas and the land of Oz were sufficiently far away not to keep me awake at night, but Darby O'Gill lived just down the road, somewhere in Ireland; and his world of leprechauns and banshees was outside my window at night.

No matter how corny the characters in the picture postcard parish of Rathcullen, I recognised the fields, I knew the smell of Guinness from drunk men's breath, and my father wore a cap just like Darby O'Gill's.

I do not recall much of the plot but all through childhood and beyond I have remained haunted by vivid remembered images: little leprechauns in mad underground celebration dancing round pots of gold, leaping over plundered treasures; Michael and Katy skipping hand in hand through the fields; the jaunty, laughing, Guinness swilling, devil may care Darby with his pub stories, his sideways philosophy and his battles of wit with the wily King Brian of the leprechauns; but mainly, and most frighteningly, the dreaded death coach with its headless coachman come to call Darby's soul on the one way trip to hell. The thought of it still sends shivers throughout me. Therein is part of the magic of cinema: to implant a visual image so strong that somewhere in the psyche the cinematic illusion becomes as real or as powerful as any actual experience.

Hollywood sends back its version of Irish folklore and legend and we buy it with added Technicolor and schmaltz. Put it in the shop window in New York on St Patrick's Day along with forty shades of green paperweights, the lacquered shillelaghs, and the wonderful world of dee-deelee eedeelee eedeelee Irishness; skipping dancing jolly little leprechauns in bright buckled shoes and battered hatted bow legged bright red drunken faced gombeen men with little devils in their laughing Irish eyes, mischievous gossipy white haired old women with shawls, pure white skinned colleens skipping carefree through green fields dutifully ready to return in an instant to domestic chores, strapping athletic lads with fine belts and sturdy boots ever willing to put in a fair day's work or hit each other a clout.

I suppose when they string together every possible Celtic cliché, you can only sit back and submit knowing that the stereotype is so overplayed as to be utterly ridiculous, yet at the same time resenting the perpetration of it.

While wanting to dismiss the stereotyping and silly superstition, the snag remains that within all the ballyhoo there are elements of truth. So instead of being outraged, one is left with a resigned smirk. How can *Darby O'Gill* be dismissed as superstitious nonsense when it is part descriptive of a society where even now devotional queues are forming to watch supposedly moving statues. If there is a bit of a want about such people then the good Catholic church surely provides for it. Miracles and dramatic visions, wonderful and fearful, are the stuff on which the faith has survived. The interweave of religion, superstition and legend within Irish history and culture is a living interrelationship which has not died with the coming of any modern age.

Exaggeration is an integral part of the Irish storytelling and myth making tradition and any tale will be followed by the remark 'sure that's nothin' ' from an unimpressed listener who will then proceed to recall or invent an even more amazing yarn. The whiskey glass from which King Brian drank is given pride of place as a hallowed relic on the top shelf of The Rathcullen Arms, destined to be the basis of many a tall tale. It is no coincidence that we move from this shot to a view of the holy pictures and medals surrounding Katy's mirror.

Darby O'Gill serenades King Brian © Walt Disney Productions

And then there was the re-view. If it was like seeing a long lost friend again after twenty-seven years, *Darby O'Gill* was comfortingly predictable with touches of the old sparkle but we had lost a lot of common ground as I had moved from a place of romance and innocence through a world of cynicism and calculated sophistication. Every technical device and dramatic trick was blatantly obvious this time through, and yet there was still a lot of delight, not from smug recognition of prize kitsch, but for a good yarn well told with the perfect characterisation of Albert Sharpe in the title role. If you are talking of definitives you are talking of Olivier as Richard III, Charles Laughton as the Hunchback of Notre Dame, W C Fields as Mr Micawber, Phil Silvers as Ernie Bilko, and Albert Sharpe as Darby O'Gill. His bright eyed, dishevelled, toothless, likeable, harmless old rogue is a cinematic gem, crucial to the enjoyment of the whole film by providing an almost believable character focus in the midst of crudely painted cardboard mountains, fake Irish accents, and stick on red sideburns.

What was once awesome fantasy all seems rather tame now. The magical world of Darby O'Gill was shattered long ago when television came into the houses of Carrickfergus. The Ideal had to close down, and a vandal's brick made it the Id al, which spelled the end of an era.

(JOHN CARSON)

I remember a cinema full of screaming kids giving the 'fuck off' V sign to a newsreel of Winston Churchill giving his 'victory' V sign. Later I understood why our national hero was so unpopular: he was the Tory minister who had called out the troops against the miners in the 1920s, an action much more pertinent in our mining town than the defeat of Hitler.

(MICHAEL O'PRAY)

CLIPPED DIALOGUE

Approaching the 60 watt twilight, rocking on your heels at the leaden doors, your reason already gone into reverse as you pad across the spongey carpet. Then the skinny fey usher in white gloves neatly snips your proffered ticket in two: with a pair of nail scissors.

Midway through the film the houselights come up, the screen goes dark. Three men have forced their way in. They make their way to the front and start peering, aggressively, into the faces of row upon row of startled punters. In the

paranoid, anguished silence you surmise, or maybe you were told later, that these heavies have been swindled in some drug deal in the scuzzy wine lodge next door, and that they are out to commit violence against the perpetrator. For a long moment you, and each and every one of your neighbours, pray that you are not this man's doppelgänger. More or less satisfied we're not, the howling lowlife departs. But we can't settle.

(PAUL HAMMOND)

DAD

Some of the front seats on the other side of the aisle were occupied by a gang of Teds. They took little interest in the film and just larked about. Next to us sat a man and his two children. I have this image of them being very poor. He wore a cap and a longish mac done up at the neck. The man asked the Teddy boys to be quiet. He asked them a few times. They stood up, laughed and fooled around. The man finally stood up and went over to them imploring them to be quiet. I remember his children becoming very agitated. It was then he was stabbed. He stood there slightly bent for a few seconds holding his stomach and then he staggered and slowly fell to the floor.

(RALPH HAWKINS)

DOUBLE DEATH

Custer of the West climaxes with a reconstruction of the celebrated Battle of Little Big Horn. Kirk Douglas in the title role finally stands alone on the battlefield in the midst of his dead troops, and exposed to the arrows of the Indians who circle round him. Yet he is not to die: at the very last moment the image jumps slightly and then we note Custer's singular *absence* at the centre of the famous circle, which at that moment begins to break up. Disappeared, literally, without a trace. Obviously caused by a simple technical fault, this spiriting away of his death gave him a singular nobility totally lacking from the rest of the film.

(PETR KRAL)

PUTTING BACK THE RITZ

Between about 1947 and 1951, when the Ritz in Sheffield, Alabama was still open, my main encounters with the place — between the ages of four and eight — were on trips with my father across the river to pick up the final reports on the daily receipts on all four of the Rosenbaum theatres our family owned in Sheffield and Tuscumbia. (There were three more in Florence at the end of his route, and two more in Athens, where he drove once a month.) As soon as we left Florence and crossed the Tennessee River we passed from Lauderdale, a dry county, to Colbert, a wet one, and the difference was plainly visible: a sudden array of beerstands and gaudy neon nightclubs flickering past made Sheffield a sort of Baghdad next to the more prim outposts in Florence, the birthplace of W C Handy, and a bastion of respectability.

Sheffield was the smaller town, but it had a bigger train station, more industrial soot, more prostitutes, and an all black movie house, the Carver, all in close proximity to one another. Across the tracks was 'Jack's Chicken Shack', a Negro hangout that sold bootleg liquor after the county went dry around 1952, and Sheffield began to grow more ashen and dusty, shrivelling into a near semblance of a ghost town.

Today the town shows some signs of coming back to life. Colbert went wet again in 1982, there's an active local theatre group, and some people in the area are in the process of restoring and reopening the Ritz — which had survived mainly as a warehouse, and briefly as a recording studio in 1957 — putting on plays, and possibly a film series too. It hasn't shown a movie for over thirty years, but

When I read Milton's description in *Paradise Lost* **of Satan, fallen to lie in Hell, a monstrous unimaginable bulk, I was reminded of that Odeon.**

(ROLAND MILLER)

If you live in the
Aussie outback you
need all the friends
you can get. When I
saw my friend Bob
Hope in some comedy
or other at the age of
six I provided him
with an imaginary
wife, who was called
'Nothing'. I don't
mean she didn't have
a name; that was her
name: 'Nothing'. You
can see I had no great
hopes for my future
as a woman.

(DEIRDRE CLARK)

the pink seashell murals, the stage, and the 'white' and 'coloured' balconies are still intact: fossils of another culture.

My father's nightly trips across the river were usually to the Colbert in Sheffield (built around the time of Pearl Harbour, half a block from the Ritz, today a parking lot) and the Tuscumbian (built in 1950, a block from the Strand, today part of a bank). But if the daily figures hadn't yet been brought over from the Ritz and Strand, he would stop off there too. Sometimes my brothers and I were allowed to get out of the car with him and peek at the movie in progress while he spoke to the manager or cashier. In a way it functioned for us like window shopping: a random five minute slice of a feature would enable us to decide whether to see the whole thing at the Shoals, Princess or Majestic in Florence, when it resurfaced there.

But sometimes a double bill would show at the Ritz and nowhere else. One such occasion was Labor Day 1949, when my parents went off on a holiday barbecue or picnic and deposited the three oldest boys — David (eight), Jonny (six) and Alvin (four) — with a teenage black babysitter named Earl at the Ritz to see *Li'l Abner* (the early black and white version, with Buster Keaton in a small part) and *I Married a Witch*. It was Alvin's first time at the movies, but the other three of us were seasoned veterans by this time. Jim Crow laws dictated that we all sit up in the coloured balcony, so we followed Earl up the stairs of the separate entrance, located to the right of the box office, and found ourselves in the highest tier of the auditorium. Down below were the pink seashell murals lit by fluorescent lights, and distant black and white movies on the screen. *Li'l Abner* — without the colour of the comic strip in the Sunday paper — seemed bogus, and bogus hillbilly at that; but David and Earl, both schooled in the macho preference for raucous art, liked nothing better than a bogus barnyard. For Alvin and me, bogus mansions and graveyards were the thing, and *I Married a Witch* a sweeter brew.

The principal moment I'm left with is a shot of two smoky essences in bottles, the sound of dry autumn leaves rustling through a chill night wind, and the voices of Cecil Kellaway and Veronica Lake, father and daughter, conversing from their adjacent bottles. Most of this has to do with Veronica Lake's deep, husky voice: a smoky spirit whose name and form collectively conjured up a feminine aura of water, vapour, air, smoke and flesh at the same time; a floating dreamboat that any boy of six would be proud to be married to. Having just seen *Topper* at the Princess the week before, I had all I needed to complete my erotic evaporation fantasies. Indeed, by the time that the credits of René Clair's supernatural comedy came on, the ads had already done their work, and I was already invisibly inside that bottle too, ready to share in Veronica's throaty vibrato.

(JONATHAN ROSENBAUM)

SIX PENN'ORTH OF DARK

In the 1930s you learnt how to behave as a human being from movies. You learnt how to smoke, how to hold a cigarette. I wanted to become a reporter because I lusted after a belted trenchcoat like the one Joel McCrea wore in Hitchcock's *Foreign Correspondent*. Girls kissed with their eyes closed and raising themselves up on tiptoe, because that was the cute shot in American movies. We believed in Hollywood. Cinemas themselves were special. Nobody had central heating, so it was warm. It was dark: 'six penn'orth of dark' was what people were after. The cinema was our motel. And it was opulent in the way nothing else in your life was. They were called 'picture palaces' for a very good reason. At the Empire, Leicester Square, the toilets were truly lavish: 'I dreamt I dwelt in marble halls' had real meaning. Before the cinema opened the men on the staff were given cigars to puff, so that when you came into the foyer it had that smell of luxury.

There were staff rackets. Teas were served in cinemas then. When you wanted tea you could either have a pot of tea, or a 'cinema tea', which was a pot of tea and a plate on which was a sandwich with the crusts cut off, which also represented something, and a cake. It's very difficult to eat in the dark. We noticed that quite often if people ate the

Originally a concert hall in which Liszt played and Dickens read, Cork's Assembly Rooms then became a cinema. The usher's name was George, and during the westerns whenever a redskin bit the dust the audience called out, 'Georgie, take out the body!' When the Assembly closed the story goes that they found hundreds of dead Indians behind the screen.

(MICK HANNIGAN)

sandwich they left the cake, or vice versa, so when we used to collect the trays from them we would take whatever was left. At the back of the stalls there were radiators which had plush curtains and we would shove these cakes and sandwiches under the radiators, and the next time somebody ordered a 'cinema tea' we would go to the kitchen and order a pot. Maybe the 'cinema tea' was 9d and the pot of tea was 6d. We'd then pull out a sandwich and a cake, put it on the tray: nobody could see what they were eating, and we'd pocket the difference. The stuff could have been under there for days, if not weeks. I remember in the RAF at Blackpool going to the pictures, and they didn't bother with an intermission. Tea was served at 4.30 no matter what was happening. Suddenly the film would stop. The lights would go up and they would serve tea. What you quickly learned was not to sit on the end of the row, because the usherettes would pass the trays down the row and as soon as everybody was served they'd give the nod to the projectionist, the lights would go down again, and on the film would go. When people had drunk their tea they would pass the trays to the end of the row. If you were sitting there you would have to peer over the pile of cups on your lap.

There were other tricks you could pull. You regularly turned the heating up before the intermission, when the icecream girl appeared. If there was anything like a Foreign Legion story, or something like Hitchcock's *Lifeboat*, when the characters had to ration out the water, you'd slowly turn up the heat.

There were girls who couldn't walk backwards. Some usherettes couldn't carry the icecream trays: 'I can't do it, Mr Norden, I come over funny if I walk backwards.' You wondered what genetic quirk there was. I was only seventeen and the girl would say, 'I can't do the ice creams today, it's my time of month.' Ten days later she'd say, 'I can't do it, it's my time of month.' I didn't know enough about the subject to be able to query it.

I was at the Trocadero, Elephant and Castle, as an assistant manager, and there were a hundred and twenty-two on the staff. It was military, everyone in uniform, and there was a staff parade. The manager would inspect the ranks. You had to stand with your hands held out, and he'd

The Honorary Consul: a slow, moody, almost mute film. At one point our hero, drunk, mindless, ruined in body and spirit, crashes to the muddy ground, a monument to excess. From the other side of the wafer-thin wall between Odeon One and Two comes the voice of *The Jungle Book*'s Baloo: 'I want to *talk* like you, *walk* like you, I want to *be* like you.'
(CHRIS PROCTOR)

look at your nails. The public paid to see gleaming buttons, luxury. Everything had to preserve the illusion. For example, we were not allowed to show 'white screen'. When the curtains part and you see a white screen you know you're watching a screen and it isn't real. So projectionists had to put a colour tint onto the screen before the first frame hit. It was showmanship so that the illusion might have force, impact.

The Saturday morning club for kids was murder. I had to announce a big disaster during the war, the fall of France or something, and it was during a children's matinee. We had to tell them because they might have wanted to go home. It was Christmas time, and we used to give them oranges and sweets. This bad news had come through, and of course nobody had television then; not everybody had a radio. Maybe it was Narvik, although now I can't even remember what Narvik was. The place was full: twelve hundred kids. So I said to the organist, whose name was Bobby Page, 'I'll come up on the organ.' I announced: 'We've had this bad news'. And the kids all shouted, 'Where's the fucking oranges! Where's the fucking oranges!'

Cinema manager grooms himself before the main feature

Unshelled peanuts: after the second house the floor was audible. You walked audibly. It was like the whole audience was eating celery. I had a mate who could crack peanuts between his knees, which was an enormous asset if you had a girl with you.

At the Watford Gaumont, which I managed, people would come in dinner dress and they would have the same seat every week. (A) you had to remember their name, and greet them by name; and (B) you had to remember their seat. As a cinema manager you thought up your own publicity stunts. If the film was, say, *Old Mother Riley Goes to Paris*, you'd have three of your doormen dressed up as Old Mother Riley, which was a very cheap costume to hire, and you'd build an Eiffel Tower, put it on a barrow and go round the town during the busy shopping time. You'd give prizes of tickets. You'd run competitions. You'd do 'tie-ins' with the local shops: you'd sell the Paris idea to them for instance. There was a magazine called *Kine Weekly*, which would give a showman's award for the best stunt.

At the Trocadero there were gangs. The tenement slums at Elephant and Castle have since disappeared. The gangs were called up during the war. But before that they used to raid. They'd try and 'bump in'. One of them bought a ticket and he'd go to an exit, open the door and his mates would flood in. These gangs were thirty- and forty-strong, youths in long black overcoats and white knotted scarves, like Sid Field. It was your job to chuck 'em out. There were pitched battles, so they lay in wait for you. I took over from a guy who went out the stage door and somebody said to him, 'Have you got a light?' As he put his hand in his pocket he was grabbed from behind and they razored his face. I used to go back home via the local Underground and I'd take six of our Irish doormen with me, all of them six foot three, and they'd take the rollers from the roller towels in the Gents and they'd stand around me, and we would go out in a 'flying wedge'. These were tough people. The gangs would want to watch the film, but occasionally also drag an usherette into the exit. They'd barricade themselves in. We had a couple of usherettes raped. We'd ring up the police, who would take a bunch of these youths into the same exit and do 'em over. At the Troc we had a list of troublemakers, plus police photographs, nicknames and descriptions, above the cashier's grille. There was one lady called 'Toss-Off Kate' who used to go round the audience and sit beside various isolated gentlemen and ask them if they wanted to be serviced. What I liked about her was that she charged less in the 6ds than she did in the 1/3s: she had a sliding scale.

At the Trocadero there were always six hundred people waiting in the 6d queue. We did four shows a day. As we took one house in the queue would form again. An enormous bomb fell on a place nearby called Spurgeon's Tabernacle, so close that it blew in all the windows and knocked the marquee for six. Nobody left the queue: they weren't going to lose their place, they'd been queueing for an hour. People came anticipating a double feature. They'd ring me up and say, 'What's the also?' You had two films, the first feature and then the 'also'. We got top West End variety acts. We had an orchestra, an organ, two major feature films, all for 6d. We did opera. We played circuses

The auditorium of the Holloway Odeon hit by a V2 rocket, August 1944

there. The stage was wide but it had no depth. When we had the circus the lions were put behind the screen, but we were showing an MGM picture and every time the lion at the beginning roared the lions at the back would answer him.

I was a relief manager, sent around the Gaumont circuit. At the Troxy, in Commercial Road, Stepney, they'd have American stars coming over. One big American came out to do his act and I saw him blanch, and then visibly pull himself together before proceeding. I went round afterwards and asked him what was the problem. He said, 'I've never seen anything like this.' It was an early show. He had to come on and be funny at 1.30 in the afternoon. And the whole front row was full of women who were breastfeeding their babies.

Cinemas had their own magazines: the Gaumont, Watford, had its own magazine; the State, Kilburn, had its own magazine, and I used to write for them and did verses. It was a community. People would ring up and say, 'Can you get Mrs So-and-So, her baby's crying and I can't stop her.' So you'd write a carbon-backed slide with this message and project it over the film. And then you'd hear scurrying feet in the cinema. I started writing organ solos. A cinema organ is like a big jelly mould, illuminated from within, a most spectacular thing that changed colour according to whether a major key or a minor key was being played. I would write parodies of popular songs and my selection would go all around the circuit. I thought I was Terence Rattigan.

On a Sunday night you used to show different films from the rest of the week. You'd show films that were old, even in those days. One Sunday at the Trocadero the chief circle usher said to me, 'I think you'd better come up to the back circle, Gents, we've got a bloke behaving obscenely.' So I went up and there was a bloke standing in the middle of the toilets, by the basin, tossing himself off, and I said, 'What do you think you're doing?' He said, 'I can't help it.' We were showing a Jessie Matthews film called *Evergreen*, one of her first films, in which she wore long silk stockings. He said, 'When I was a kid I saw that film, and I wanked for days on end. And I've come back years later and it's had the same effect on me.'

While the trailers trailed Anne visited the Ladies, then returned groaning and limping. She'd misjudged the weight of the chromium door and crushed her big toe. Marty visited the Gents and returned, groaning and holding his head. He'd misjudged the size of the chromium door and knocked himself flat. Nursing our wounds, clutching foot and forehead, the film began. *Aliens*: **'This Time It's War.'**

(MARTY ST JAMES & ANNE WILSON)

The legs of Jessie Matthews in Evergreen

The habit of going to see the movie — that sophisticated notion — no, people went to 'the pictures', they didn't go to see such-and-such a film. 'What are you doing Tuesday night?' 'Going to the pictures.'

(Denis Norden)

WITH A FIGURE LIKE YOURS

I cannot recall the number of occasions I shuffled back in regulation sex cinema garb to see *Daughters of Darkness*, the lesbian vampire movie that starred Delphine Seyrig as Countess Erzsébet Báthory and Andrea Rau as her lover Ilona. In those days I lived with my parents and when the film resurfaced at a local cinema I convinced them to spend an evening feasting their eyes on those sanguinary sapphics.

My father had purchased a box of Maltesers, the chocolates with the less fattening centre, to sustain him through this no holds barred erotic horror film. With my mother we settled down in the back row. My father quickly fell asleep. He chanced to resurface at a moment in the film when the divine Ms Rau is indulging in carnal acrobatics with the leading male actor. As she pouted and sighed, locked in an impossible sexual position, my father's leg jerked involuntarily, catapulting the Maltesers onto the floor.

The cinema was bereft of carpets and we all could hear, for what seemed an eternity, was the doleful roll of each Malteser down the incline to its nemesis beneath the feet of the people in the front row. Not only was the rumble of the sweeties heard by the audience. On the screen the actor had reached orgasm. Then he turned his head to one side as if he, too, was listening to the Maltesers rolling past the front row, under the bed on which he and Andrea had cavorted, towards the French windows on the far side of his bedroom, and out into the garden.

(CHARLES PELTZ)

NOT IN YOUR HAND

For Simon and me, short light coloured macs, mohair sweaters, slim jim ties, tight trousers and chisel toed shoes were obligatory for our adolescent cultural trips to the cinema. The films were inevitably foreign and subtitled, and even if we didn't understand them it was as though through exposure to some cinematic photosynthesis we would absorb the esoteric and become all the better intellectually for it.

On one occasion, to kill time before a suitably uplifting film, we met at Waterloo station and decided to go to the cinema within the station precinct which showed a continuous programme of cartoons for the convenience of passengers with time on their hands. This was not entirely true of the matronly middle aged woman and her elderly male companion sitting three seats away from me, as she applied herself methodically to his penis. What intrigued me was their mutual indifference to an activity I'd always imagined to be both intimate and passionate. As she ate

Have you ever been the only punter in a big cinema? The film has been showing to an empty room. Now there is you. Eventually, guilty about being there, you leave. Does the film continue to the end?

(IAN WALKER)

In Diner Mickey Rourke bets his buddies that the sophisticated lady will hold his penis on their first date. He pokes it through the bottom of the popcorn box they share. She has a healthy appetite. He wins the bet

Maltesers from the box on her knee, apparently engrossed in the antics of Mickey Mouse, Donald Duck or Pluto her left hand seemed not to know what her right was doing. It felt inappropriate that my introduction to live sex was wholly voyeuristic and accompanied by images from *Looney Tunes*.

(CHARLIE HOLMES)

FAMILY ENTERTAINMENT

Carol, who went to see *Jungle Book*, has a daughter, so her child is not David, who ate the popcorn. *Snow White* was the main feature at the cinema where the choc ice was eaten. Ann bought the hot dog, so Carol, who did not buy the ice lolly, must have bought the orangeade. So *Tom and Jerry* must have been the support film for *Jungle Book*. Therefore Carol's daughter is not Julie, whilst Donna was taken to see *Mary Poppins*, so it must have been Linda who went with Carol to see *Jungle Book*. We know that David's mother is neither Carol nor Ann, who bought the popcorn, nor is she Jean, whilst Meg is Simon's mother, so David's mother must be Helen, and they therefore saw *Mickey Mouse*. We know that they did not see *Jungle Book* and *Popeye* was the supporting item for *Peter Pan*. As David ate popcorn, he did not see *Snow White*, and we know that Donna watched *Mary Poppins*, so Helen and David must have seen *Fantasia*. *Mary Poppins* was not supported by *Bugs Bunny*, so Donna must have seen Donald Duck leaving *Bugs Bunny* as the cartoon screened with *Snow White*. Therefore Ann's child, who did not see *Donald Duck*, cannot be Donna, and must be Julie, who therefore ate the hot dog. The film combination rules out Donna as the child who ate the choc ice, so Meg and Simon must have watched *Snow White* and *Bugs Bunny*, leaving Donna as the eater of the ice lolly. By elimination, Donna's mother must be Jean, and the programme seen by Ann and Julie must have been *Peter Pan* and *Popeye*.

(CHARLIE HOLMES)

UNCLE SAM

Until I was eight I lived in the village of Feltwell in Norfolk where there was a joint RAF and USAF base. Although the RAF children came to the local primary school there was little contact between us locals and the American children. However on Saturday mornings there was a film show, run by the Americans for their children, which the local children could also attend. I went once, when I was five. I remember nothing about who I was with or what the films were, I remember only the interval. Members of the audience were invited to participate in some games. I volunteered along with four or five others. An American soldier gave us each a balloon and told us that the winner would be the one who could soonest burst the balloon by blowing it up beyond its stretching point. We all started to inflate our balloons and eventually one burst. It was not over then however, as the soldier said that the rest of us should continue until we had also burst our balloons. One by one everyone else's balloon burst but I lacked the courage to blow too hard. The soldier, becoming bored with the game, laconically reached out his cigarette end and burst the balloon in my face.

Thirty years later my volunteering instinct has come through intact but I still mistrust the American Air Force.

(VIEANNE LYLE)

FIRST WESTERN IN THE EAST

A small cinema on a Royal Air Force camp near the Egyptian town of Suez in 1951. A crowd of people filled the darkened space with noise and smoke. Other noisy people who were very grey moved rapidly backwards and forwards on the end wall. These people, one of whom was a whiskered old man, carried guns which they let off frequently, rode horses at terrifying speeds across an arid landscape similar to the one I played in each day, while breathless crashing music and a small dog pursued every- one everywhere they went. Suddenly all this stopped and blinding bright lights came on. As I was swept along by the noisy laughing crowd out into the tropical evening I persistently wanted to know what had happened to the dog. For several nights afterwards nightmares of violence and death disturbed normally peaceful sleep.

A few days later the emergency evacuation of civilians from Suez to within the camp's barbed wire perimeter fence began. Hand guns were issued to all personnel guarding the convoys of lorries. At the end of each day my father would return, a holster on his hip. The pistol would be discreetly locked away in a cupboard. Soon afterwards we were all evacuated by air, back to England. Later I learned the old man was Gabby Hayes and the film starred Roy Rogers.

(MIKE LEGGETT)

My friend was followed from seat to seat by a dirty old man during *He-Man and the Masters of the Universe*. She'd soon had enough of this and yelled out, 'I am She-Ra and I will break your balls!' That did the trick.

(GERRY McCARTHY)

GATEWAY TO THE STARS

It was a life-size cutout of Roy Rogers on Trigger that held me. It stood in the entrance to the cinema: the stetson, white suit, palomino horse, silver spurs. I kept wondering what it had to do with the cowboy we were going to see on the screen. Similarly, I remember peering through the expanded grille they drew across the cinema entrance when it was closed. Although the movie had ended they, the stars, were still visible in the publicity stills behind glass, just inside the entrance. I was fascinated by these glossy black and white photographs. I couldn't understand how these moments had become frozen in time like that. Had they literally cut them out of the film? Once, a still photograph had slipped from its frame, and lay enticingly just inside the gate. I reached through one of the diamond shaped gaps between the bars and pulled the curling portrait out. It felt illicit. I was stealing something out of the film: I had captured the stars in the act, and they couldn't slip away, off the edge of the screen.

From the age of eight I attended the Odeon in Exeter. It was the second largest building in the city, next to the cathedral, which was much less prominent. The Odeon dominated from the highest point in Exeter, surrounded by terraced houses like regular furrows in a ploughed field. There it crouched, hump backed on the hill, overshadowing everything round about, a Behemoth. I suppose I had been given a sense of the evil of cinema by my strict Methodist grandparents, who were visibly shocked when once I confessed that I had been to see a film on Sunday.

Inside the Odeon, on both sides of the screen, up the soaring walls, ran a frieze of cartoon characters. They seemed to ascend two giant rainbows: Snow White and her Dwarfs, Mickey and Minnie, Pluto, Donald and his nephews, Popeye and Olive. I remember these figures illuminated from behind, like giant shadows. It was as though they were marching up great soaring bridges to get on to the screen, where they would enter into the films we had come to see. Then there were the sweeping layers of thin gauzy curtains that swished elegantly back to reveal the screen. Sometimes this happened after the film had

In a dream I went to the pictures, in Germany I think. I paid in gold coins and got change in jewels, amethysts in gold mounts. The audience sat in a warm honey glow, drinking tea and eating richly iced cake. You appeared on screen, pretending to be a bush, a bush with round purplish leaves and pale green shoots.

(P P O'Leary)

begun, when the curtains rippled the frame round the black and white British film censor's certificate, like a giant bank note.

I could never get over the transformation of the vast auditorium by the dimming of the lights, the beautiful changes of colour on the curtains, and the anticipation brought on by the roaring lion, the muscle man with his gong, the snow capped mountain, the searchlights probing the 20th Century. That moment seems in retrospect to have been more exciting than any of the films that followed. The 20th Century Fox logo always made me think we were about to see a war film, as the searchlights that had woken us in London in the blitz always preceded an air-raid. Even in peace time Exeter, bombed London, in reality and on the newsreels, was hard to dislodge from my mind.

(ROLAND MILLER)

THE FACTS OF LIFE

The three major cinematic events in my life have functioned as harbingers to major changes in my own life, after which things were never quite the same.

The first one, the first time in fact that I can remember going to the pictures, was being taken to the cinema in Lewisham by my mother to see *Snow White and the Seven Dwarfs* just before the outbreak of the Second World War. For a child of five this was a terrifying experience, although it was meant to be a birthday treat. The fact that it had a happy ending was immaterial to me. As far as I was concerned it was a nightmare, and merged in my memory with actually being evacuated; the kids going down to Ladywell station in a crocodile on one side of the road, clutching oranges and bars of chocolate, and the mothers on the other, weeping and wailing and shouting to us across the street, lots of dwarfs and lots of Snow Whites.

The second one: having got over the actual evacuation and the idea that I probably wouldn't ever see my mother

On screen *Peeping Tom*. Possessed by the movie camera with which his sadistic father tortured him in childhood 'Tom' skewers his girlfriend with a stiletto tripod leg while he films the grim business. My companion leaps from his seat and himself shoots the scene with his Bolex. An umbilicus is being tugged.

(DAVID CURTIS)

again, being evacuated in itself was great. Our school was evacuated to Hadlow Down in Sussex, just about where the German bombers used to off-load their bombs to save themselves the trouble of having to go all the way to London. There were a lot of French-Canadian soldiers stationed in the area, together with British and Americans, and a weekly film show was put on for all-comers in the Methodist chapel on Saturday nights. The first, and only, film that I can remember seeing there was *Sergeant York*, the dialogue of which was very loudly interpreted by the more bilingual of the French-Canadians for their monoglot mates, much to the annoyance of the anglophones. I think also that aspersions were cast, as asides, on the true soldierly qualities of Sgt York, and hence on all American soldiers, and a three-way fight broke out among the French-Canadian, American and British, to a background drone of German bombers wending their weary way to or from London, or circling in a desultory fashion prior to dumping their bombs with a dull thud on the surrounding country-side. The very next day, Sunday, I would have to attend the same chapel in its religious function, and the fact that the previous evening it had been a battleground for people who were supposed to be friends and allies, while the 'enemy' got on with his job uninterrupted outside, led to a more or less permanent confusion in my mind, which I now believe to be totally justified, between violence and religion, and between fact and fancy (or film).

The third one: once the buzz bombs started to come over it was at last realised that it wasn't a very good idea to have children evacuated directly on the flight path between Germany and London, and we were all shipped off to other locations, myself to Teignmouth in Devon. There, in the only cinema, we had a sadistic manager who delighted in not letting the kids into 'A' films unless we could con a grown-up into buying the tickets and going in with us, after which we would split up and go our separate ways, ourselves to the front row if possible, otherwise as near to the screen as we could get. But on one mysterious occasion the sado-manager waived the rules and waved us in: we couldn't understand this behaviour at all, but took up the offer nevertheless, putting it down to grown-up incon-

A grim, angst-filled film by Ingmar Bergman became ludicrously enjoyable through the persistent hiccups of the person sitting in front of me, which provided a perfect counterpoint to the strangulated Swedish voices onscreen.

(GEORGE LITTLEBLACK)

Cinema in Buchenwald

sistency. The programme took its usual course, until it came to news time. The wartime commentator's jingoistic jangle was this time replaced by a solemn voice, and we were confronted with pictures of moving skeletons, some of them smiling weakly and making slow gestures. This was the newsreel of the liberation of Belsen, and I think that I have thought about those images every day since. Before that I had never known that human beings could do such things to others, but after that I knew.

(JOHN FURNIVAL)

WEEPING

As in a waiting room I sit. Surrounded by breathing, close enough to neighbours to touch knees. The seats are cushioned, and in the dark I am waiting for more than entertainment. I am waiting to be bathed in film. It is a matinee performance of *ET The Extra-Terrestrial*. I am not lost in the story, it is like reading a comic on the bus. Children chatter loudly. What are they talking about? Anything and everything. A conference hall for the under elevens. Towards the end of the film attention is gradually transferred to the screen. Sadder things are happening. ET is homesick. He might die. I am jarred by the sound of these children weeping.

(FRANKIE EARNSHAW)

THE PASSENGER

That shadowy world of small rooms visited by regret, of dim streets crossed by half familiar figures, of meadows steeped in yearning, beckoned to me. There must have been a draught because I wrapped my coat around my knees. As I left the cinema I was seized in an irresistible spasm of shivering. My jaw hurt, my teeth were locked in an instinctive bite, and when released they chattered as if propelled by clockwork. It took ten minutes of brisk walking to get my blood flowing again, my consciousness slowly returning from a journey beyond my body. I boarded a train. The suburban setting of my destination was unexceptional, simply a footbridge over tracks, a few solemn railway buildings, a row of villas, a couple of trees. And yet, alighting in the sunshine from the trembling train I found myself in a space transfigured by the three stages of the passage through the underworld that is matinee cinema: the transition from day to night; the day for night of the viewing; the transition back to daylight.

(ROGER CARDINAL)

Photomontage by Ian Breakwell, 1980

UM AL-MARHOOM'S SHADOW

I was six years old and had to be accompanied to the cinema by my two brothers (five and seven). They had refused to go with me, claiming they wouldn't be able to face their friends after that. My father threatened to punish them, so they were forced to accept my company. The cinema we went to was the Al Washash summer cinema, situated in Baghdad City. We had to be there one hour before the beginning of the film in order to get seats in the front row. Following our father's advice both brothers made sure I was seated between them, at the same time refusing to exchange a word with me.

It was inevitable that I was fully occupied by my fear rather than watching an Egyptian film, *Abla and Anter*, a classic Bedouin love story. Half an hour later an ambiguous shadow covered the screen, then manifested a distinct movement. At once I turned my head to the source of the light. My eldest brother told me to keep still. The same shadow kept covering the screen at regular intervals. Shrinking into my seat I murmured, 'It has to be God.' Or was it part of the film?

Ten years later I discovered while watching the same film on TV that the shadow wasn't part of the film after all:

it was Um Al-Marhoom's shadow (Um Al-Marhoom is what we in the Middle East call the woman who is left without children after the death of her only son), trying to sell some boiled chickpeas to us children.

(HAIFA ZANGANA)

WHITE SQUARE

I remember watching flecks in the concrete passing under the tips of my black button shoes and the flaked brown paint of the step of my pushchair. Then some grass, and a dark green van, and doors opening at the back of it, and grey flat people moving in a white square. Must have been the early 1940s, my mother taking me for a walk near Bostall Woods during a gap in the bombing. Some Ministry of Something travelling information film. Towards the end of the war another memory. A trip to London to visit my 'Aunt' Josie. A bigger white square. A man playing a ukulele and riding a bicycle across the sky. Then a live magician on the stage; some singing; the flat white again and men firing rifles across dead buffalo at the rest of the herd. Afterwards I sat on the mat that smelled of dog while my mother and Josie talked. About Josie's son drowned at sea and her daughter Irma's fiancé 'missing'. He was in the Fleet Air Arm. I liked those words and repeated them often to myself.

(TOM RAWORTH)

SNAKE SCALE

As a kid the scale of the film images was frightening, and then there were the myriads of dots, scratches and lines, accompanied by clicks and plops on the soundtrack. I remember trying to make sense out of these ghostly darting signs that overlaid the story of the film, which most of the time I couldn't follow. When I was older, eight or nine, I used to take a large piece of plasticine to the pictures and make what was appropriate. Once, during a jungle film I made a snake by rolling out the plasticine on the back of the seats. At a particularly exciting point I dropped it between the seats in front, and insisted that my parents ask the people to look for it. After some time, and the lighting of matches, I got the snake back covered in fragments of crisps, popcorn and cigarette ash.

(MAX EASTLEY)

A MOTHER TO ME

My first visit alone to a Saturday matinee at the Queens, just off the docks in Whitehaven, next to the Quay Street Roman Catholic chapel and infant school I attended. In the serial Superman was left in the final frames pushing desperately with his outstretched arms at the sides of a tunnel melting into a hot, dangerous, black treacle-like substance which threatened to engulf him. The image was awesome and utterly seductive.

My second memory is of another matinee film, but not a children's one. In its final moments a sophisticated urbane man in a nightclub is led discreetly through a back door into a room which is a mortuary run by nuns, one of whom shows him a dead body drawn out of a wall on a slab. The scene has never left me. I was seven years old or less.

In my third memory my mother takes me to see Chaplin's _Limelight_. I know she liked the theme music. I also knew then that seeing the film at a matinee on a weekday was an illicit pleasure for her. My father would not have approved. I had to be told which character was Chaplin; he was so old and looked nothing like the silent comic I knew so well.

All these memories are connected incoherently to my mother: the oozing uterine passage closing in on Superman; the dead man disclosed by nuns (so pretty and so erotically close to the nightclub); and the sadness of _Limelight_ where,

Two locals were scrutinising the forthcoming attractions outside the tiny cinema in Glenarm, Co. Antrim. 'Singapore. Do you suppose it's a western?'

(NOEL SPENCE)

65

sitting in the dark with her I knew her pleasure at the tale was different to mine, an adult one, beyond me. So much that is inexpressible in our relationship survives in memories of late afternoon empty cinemas in a small northern town in the 1950s.

(MICHAEL O'PRAY)

REVENGE OF THE 'D' STREAM

Sunday nights have always been a problem for the serious cinemagoer, since this is the night that brings out the lads whose parents don't make them go to bed early before a fresh week at school begins. One Sunday night at the Wood Green Odeon a group of youths and girls were making so much more than a tolerable racket that I eventually asked them to quieten down. Some hope. Humiliated, I decided to fetch the manager. The usherette assured me that the manager would do something about it but he was busy just then with the projectionist, so she would pass on my complaint when he came down.

After suffering another half hour of mouth farts and high-pitched giggles I was stiff with indignation: at the rabble, at the management, at my 'don't make a fuss' partner. Why does nobody else seem to care? I care. Gary Cooper cares. Marlon Brando cares. This was an occasion that required character. I'd go it alone and rid this cinema of the bums who terrorise it every Sunday night.

Striding boldly over I fired a sharp round of insults. Wounded, the punks were stunned into silence as my vitriolic invective ricocheted around the stalls. I was stopped short by torchlight in my face. At last here's justice, I thought. A black suit was stepping in to take the bodies away. 'All right you,' he said, shaking the beam in my eyes, 'Out! I've had complaints about you.'

The wild bunch were giggling helplessly as I was escorted, proud and unprotesting, to the exit. Tonto followed with the coats.

(CHRISTINE HAMMOND)

NOT THE LONE RANGER

In 1958 there was only one television in our street, and when the Lone Ranger made his weekly appearance it was like a mini-cinema in John Logue's front parlour with about twenty of us clustered round the little walnut cabinet. Our only hope for a TV of our own was our uncle John Hep who did the bins and could always be relied on for an old radio or a gramophone. One day he excelled himself, turning up with a piece of furniture the size of a large sideboard which housed the coveted television set along with a radiogram and a place to keep your records. It was corporation booty however, and it was only reasonable to expect that this early entertainment centre might not be firing on all cylinders. In fact the only parts that worked were the radio and the sound on the television. It was ours though, and Mrs Logue's parlour had been getting a bit rough lately. So we used to sit and listen and try to work out what was going on, which gave the Lone Ranger even more mystery.

Then came a very special occasion. Not only was the Ritz showing *The Lone Ranger and the Lost City of Gold* on the screen, but the Lone Ranger himself was going to make an appearance 'In Person'. My older brother and I immediately laid siege to our mother to let us go.

The first main feature we had ever seen. Fantastic! Like visiting the Sistine Chapel after having only read the Thames & Hudson *Michelangelo* in braille. Then the actual Lone Ranger appeared. He strode out onto the stage in his pale blue suit amid shouts of 'Where's Tonto?' and 'Take off your mask!' My brother and I had already discussed the possibility of this not being the real Lone Ranger but an impersonator dressed up, and when our man appeared we knew. His trousers were too baggy.

(JOHN KINDNESS)

My mother told me once that on November the fifth someone in the audience had thrown a firework at the screen and the people in the film jumped.
(MAX EASTLEY)

KEYNAS AND CHIV IN RATBY

The sign over the box office of the Majestic cinema, Ratby, Leicestershire in the mid 1950s read: 'It's warmer inside'. In summer the word 'warmer' was covered by a wooden panel, hung on nails, which read 'cooler'. Beneath this, another sign reassured us that 'This cinema is treated with DDT'.

The cinema was built on a hill, giving a natural rake to the auditorium seating. The back two rows of seats, from which every alternate arm rest had been removed, were for 'Couples Only'. At the age of nine I wondered how I would handle my eventual initiation to the back row seating. The occasion arrived in June 1960, for a screening of *Samson and Delilah*, with Victor Mature and Hedy Lamarr.

The front rows were a different world. These seats were the province of yelling, farting, belching gangs of adolescent males, the bane of the long-suffering manager, Len. It was a toss up whether to try for acceptance in the front row ranks, or work towards qualifying for the back row. One night Len's wife, a small woman, had repeatedly asked a trio of Teds from the next village to cut down their noise and stop carving the backs of the seats. On her ice cream round she lost her temper, bringing down on the head of the ringleader the entire tray of ice cream. Tubs, wooden spoons, choc ices everywhere. And silence.

In the centre of the screen was a dark, dribbled patch, a constant feature of every close up kiss, jungle scene and war torn sky. In the late 1960s I went regularly to the Plaza cinema in the Isles of Scilly. In the middle of the screen was the same dark patch.

The two most notorious characters of the Majestic front row gangs were Keynas and Chiv. Keynas was short, round, swarthy, with matt black hair and an oily burgundy Ted suit. Chiv was tall, broad, fair and clean cut, ruddy faced, shirt collar open even in the depths of winter. Keynas and Chiv were inseparable. Always in the cinema, always wise-cracking, often thrown out before the end of the film, but always back next time. Sometimes they would sit on opposite sides of the aisle so that they could turn their banter into a public performance.

'Eyup Chiv, a yo farted?'

'Wornt mey Keynas. Musta bin the bugger beyond me.'

Another night, during a close up shot of Yvonne De Carlo, Keynas called across the cinema: 'Eyup Chiv, shey's got the kinda gob tuh smoke a prick!'

And when, as often happened, the screen began to yellow and darken, the cry would go up from the front rows: 'Purra nother bob in Len!' Then Len, who was also the projectionist, would adjust the carbon rods and brightness would be restored. But if Len had nipped out the back for a smoke, the cry would go unheeded, the screen flickered and faded into blackness, then all hell would break loose. Whistling, rapid stamping, cheering, hurling of wrappers, cartons and ice creams (which would explain how the screen got stained).

Towards the end of the final reel came the scrape and swish of the velvet curtains being swept across on their metal rods, followed by the clank of the push bars and the sudden rush of cold night air down the back of the neck. A sure signal for those in the 'Couples Only' seats to adjust their dress, and the rest of us to prepare for the pre national anthem stampede. With the crescendo of the closing music the audience scrambled for the exits, leaving national servicemen and isolated royalists standing to attention. It was half a mile to the chip shop, so you had to get a head start.

I left the village in 1963. By that time the cinema had closed down, sold to a firm making fibreglass covers for pneumatic drills. From time to time I have had vivid dreams in which the Majestic has again been open for business, the glass cases full of photographs, lit up, with posters advertising wonderful movies covering the outside walls. In 1986 the plastics factory caught fire and the building was razed to the ground and the dreams have not recurred.

(CHRIS GARRATT)

TE HOKINGA MAI KI WHANGANUI

The Maori name for the New Zealand Film Archive is Nga Kaitiaki o nga Taonga Whitiahua (The guardians of treasured images of light). The most significant of the Maori films in its care are those made by James McDonald during expeditions to various parts of the country in the 1920s. The lengthy restoration process has included, besides the usual preservation and repair work, the translation of all intertitles into Maori by tribal experts, and the return of the films for screenings amongst local people.

So now after all these years we are taking *He Pito Whakaatu i Te Noho a Te Maori i Te Awa o Whanganui* (*Scenes of Maori Life on The Whanganui River*), made in 1921, back to Koroniti. It is dusk when we arrive. We are cold and cramped, and apprehensive about our reception, the adequacy of our response to the speeches of welcome, and our awful singing. But because the two meeting houses are enveloped in giant tarpaulins ready for overnight fumigation there will be no official welcome. We meet our local hosts, and in the dining room tea and lamingtons are waiting. While the equipment is being set up people come in from their work outside and visitors start arriving from up and down the Whanganui river. By the time dinner has been eaten and evening prayers conducted it is eight o'clock and about a hundred people have gathered.

There is a vocal, direct reaction to all the films on the

In the Wimpy after *2001* we imitated the apes banging their bones on the ground with our knives and forks on the formica table. 'Daaah Daaah Daaah Da! Da!' me and my brothers sang in chorus.

(MELISSA BENN)

programme. Great interest is shown in the activities and scenes depicted: the skill and panache with which cat's cradle is demonstrated is commented on, the speed and technique of the weavers astounds, the making of crayfish pots and operation of eel weirs is studied intently. The whole hall is convulsed to see children elbowed out of the way while the adults take over skipping ropes and double-dutch, 1920s style, fills the screen. There is a contemplative silence when divinatory sticks move seemingly of their own accord.

More profound and moving is the direct communication which the film opens up between the living and the dead. The children in the film are identified as the brothers and sisters of the elders among us. The adults are their parents, grandparents, aunts and uncles. Most are known by name and some are greeted as if they stood before us. The effect, though tears do flow, is not maudlin. Personal characteristics are laughed at, family likenesses in the present generations are pointed out, even among the pigs and dogs which still wander around the village.

After the film some of the elders talk to the group about the effect the films have on them, of seeing people they still feel spiritually close to on the screen, of the inheritance they have received, and the traditions they want to pass on. For some, the step back in time brings only sadness, for others what they have seen will provide an impetus for the future. We all feel touched by the greatest gift our ancestors have handed down to us. For a while there are speeches, then half the hall is up, performing song after song for us, the visitors, and for themselves as their pride in being Ngati Pamoana manifests itself.

At last the mattresses are brought out. It has been both exhilarating and draining and we have to work tomorrow, so we put in our earplugs and pull our sleeping bags over our heads while all around us the talk goes on and on.

(SHARON DELL)

Ko étehi whanganga a te Máori/Aperahama demonstrating method of measuring, Koriniti 1921. Photograph by James McDonald, courtesy National Museum of New Zealand

MIVVIS AT HIGH NOON

A day of B westerns brought in fans by the droves. Members of western clubs from all over the country converged on a private cinema in Kings Cross. Each group was dedicated to a particular cowboy, be it Red Rider, Tom Mix or Randolph Scott. Their attire was that of their hero, complete with guns and leathers. Hundreds of them assembled outside the cinema, and a group of Asian cowboys from Handsworth staged a shoot out in Grays Inn Road. Self conscious in my normal clothes I seated myself at the rear of the upper stalls.

After the first two films there was an intermission. Ice creams and soft drinks were to be served. The ice cream girl must have had a lie in this Sunday morning, and she arrived towards the end of the film showing prior to the interval. As the film ended she faced the darkened cinema. When the lights came up the girl looked at the audience, her mouth slowly opened and on her face was an expression of incredulity. The armed and thirsty outlaws were rising from their seats and moving towards her with jangling spurs and cap guns. They had one thing on their minds and she was it. The punk ice cream girl with the Mohican hair cut fled stage left.

(JOHN WELSON)

MAORI COWBOYS

In New Zealand's 'King Country' — so called because of the Maori kings who fought a guerrilla war against the settling English — Maori lads fresh from rounding up the droves of merino sheep from the bush clad hills would have a night out in the one horse town and go to the fleapit. They'd cart a case of beer and their heavy saddles into the cinema under the cloak of darkness and, sitting astride their saddles in the front row, would cheer on the cowboys and ride rough with them, Waikato 4X in one hand and their stetsons in the other. They hooped and hollered with John

Wayne, Sitting Bull, Doris Day and Jack Palance, thirsty for
the shooting and the scalping, riding hell for leather
through gorges and down hillsides. Their hats sailed up,
whirling black against the screen, as the dust rose from the
red plush seating, while in the back rows the disapproving
white 'Pakeha', the chemist, librarian, car salesman, the
dentist's wife, would shake their heads and tut tut at the
rowdies down front.

(ALYSON STONEMAN HUNTER)

MEN ON HORSEBACK

Because I found historical films about men on horseback so
moving I was pleased when my then wife, Jenni, set to
writing a book about the wild west. She wrote it in Nairobi,
where I had a university job from 1968 to 1971. It was an
exciting time, in retrospect a brief golden age between the
end of colonial rule and the point when the repressiveness
of the Kanu regime grew so blatant that disillusion,
compromise and fear became endemic. Every month or so a
new East African writer would emerge, following in the

footsteps of my already famous colleague, who then called himself James Ngugi. The first Kenyan African novelist was a man of anger, developing the marxist position that would eventually bring him detention without trial for a year, followed by exile.

After an argument about politics and poetics on the verandah of the Norfolk Hotel, I would often go with Jenni to the movies. Nairobi commonly saw Hollywood films before they reached Britain. We were not starved of new westerns in that era when great old stars were playing aged gunfighters and movie squabbled with movie on the ideological terrain laid out by the war in Vietnam.

I was captivated by *Butch Cassidy and the Sundance Kid*. Newman and Redford seemed to express the youthful, anarchical values of 1968-and-all-that. Then came a conference of the English departments of the East African universities at Moshi, in Tanzania, a wonderfully beautiful place near Mount Kilimanjaro. As wagtails flittered over the swimming pool, Jack Mitchell heard me admire Butch and lectured me sternly. Jack was a gingery Scottish communist normally domiciled in East Berlin but then teaching in Dar es Salaam. He had not been one of the late Stalin's critics, but I liked the way he sang his large repertoire of Scottish folksongs and I heeded him when he denounced Butch and Sundance.

'Arrogant American imperialism. Look, laddie, it takes the entire Bolivian Army to wipe out two gringos.'

The Wild Bunch did not seduce me. We went to see it with Ngugi and his wife Nyambura. I found the film's final frenzied violence detestable. At the end, I turned half in shame towards Ngugi, who merely grunted. I fancied that I knew what he was thinking; much like what Jack would have thought.

Back in Britain a year or two later, I was one of a panel collected to perform before a group of young Americans who were paying Richard Demarco, Edinburgh's most flamboyant cultural entrepreneur, for the privilege of drinking the wisdom of the New Scottish Enlightenment at source. The issue of violence in the arts came up. Another participant was an elderly Orcadian poetess prone to say very, very softly things such as 'life is like a glass of pure water'. When I suggested that *The Wild Bunch* was a prime example of nasty, unartistic violence, she reproved me. 'That,' she said, her voice echoing with the cries of oystercatchers and lapwings over remote beaches where seals rolled and basked inshore, '*That* is one of the most *beautiful* films ever made.'

(ANGUS CALDER)

As the credits rolled my mother and father, like most filmgoers of that generation, stood for the National Anthem. But my mother's leg had gone to sleep. It gave way beneath her, she fell and then rolled helplessly down the aisle. My father, torn between allegiance to The Wife or the Monarch, remained standing to attention, biting his stiff upper lip.

(JO FINN)

TICH'S NIGHT OUT

The Wheel Tapper pub behind the railway station in Taunton was my haven when I worked at the art college there in the late 1960s and early 1970s. Straight off the London train and in the front door. It was the one pub where students could be guaranteed not to gather in jabbering crowds: the reason was the clientele. The Wheel Tapper was a cider pub, and the only one in town that tolerated the hard core of tomato-faced cider drinkers who, outside licensing hours, sat talking garrulously on public benches or passed out surrounded by flagons on the lawns of the Floral Gardens. When the sun went down and the evening turned chill the ciderheads made for the warmth of

One day we sat there enthralled by *Hiroshima Mon Amour*. During the final minutes the woman in front of us exploded. She'd been wearing an inflatable plastic suit that slimmed your body and she'd ignited it with her cigarette.
(TOM WAKEFIELD)

the Wheel Tapper bar. At 9 o'clock I joined them. The draught cider, poured from wooden barrels, was of two kinds: sweet, which no one drank, and rough. The latter was aptly named, so tart that the first gulp curled your lips back. No one called it scrumpy, just as no one in Ireland ever says, 'Top o'the morning'. It was rough cider, known wryly as 'cripplecock' to those whose lifeblood it was. Every barrel a different strength, no quality control in those days. But never less than dangerous and unpredictable, as were its effects. A domino game was cut short when one of the players clawed his jacket to shreds trying to ward off the spiders. Another night a man rushed out of the bar and head-butted a double-decker bus. The next day a father broke his son's arm. A man playing cards had an open wound in his forehead, blood dripping onto the crib board. An old woman telling me the story of her life shat herself halfway through the Second World War. A regular in wellington boots plastered with cow dung ordered a pint, took off his overcoat and hung it up, unaware that he'd lost his trousers somewhere en route. But most nights it was quiet and uneventful. One Monday I was the only person out of four in the bar who was not unconscious. By no means the perfect pub, but as good a place as any to spend an evening in a town which I always thought would make an ideal site for a nuclear test.

Tich, my darts partner, was a loner. When the rest of the crowd turned out at closing time and headed for the Floral Gardens with their carry-outs, Tich bedded down for the night in the public lavatory on the other side of the railway bridge. On Christmas Day he was moved out by a policeman, and that, he said, was when he lost his faith. A gentle, amiable alcoholic, Tich supplemented his dole money in the pea picking season, but the soil got into the cuts on his hands and poisoned his blood. Rough cider destroys one of the healing vitamins in the body if drunk to excess, and Tich was pickled in it. His face grew puffy, his arms and legs swelled up, and his fingers turned into purple sausages so that he kept dropping his darts. They took him to the cider ward of the local hospital and a week later he was dead. But Tich was always happy in his way, and curiously one of his merriest nights was when he and the rest of the regulars didn't go to the pub.

The Shepton Mallet pop festival was one of the first and biggest outdoor pop concerts, a drug-raddled campsite without tents, populated by beaded flower children in kaftans and body paint who had hitch-hiked west in their tens of thousands. Some of them straggled back through Taunton, and being in no hurry to get home settled down in the Floral Gardens, playing guitars and tambourines, smoking joints, dropping acid and chanting mantras. The ciderheads took an instant liking to these fellow dropouts who also slept rough and were equally unsteady on their feet. But the old 'uns were scathing about the hippies' chemicals. 'You don't want to bother with none of that there marry jewarna m'dear, that's a king's ransom you'm paying. Here, have a swig of this m'old beauty, and it only be a shilling a pint.' Glug, glug, glug. 'Wow, far out, and it's organic man.' 'Oh aah, it be that all right m'dear, you'm grow leaves if you drink enough of it.'

A bond of kinship spanned the generation gap. The bar of The Wheel Tapper filled up and then one night emptied completely: *Woodstock* had eventually found its way to the local cinema. The festival film to end them all, non-stop music and a million people stoned out of their skulls. Nirvana. The hippies and the ciderheads alike were keen to see it. They formed a queue outside the cinema, pockets of greasy overcoats and grubby kaftans bulging with flagons. Those few citizens of Taunton who walked the streets after dark tut-tutted and averted their gaze as the motley queue filed inside and settled down. The film was everything they had hoped for and they loved every minute of it. The miasma of cider, dope, urine and unwashed flesh filled the auditorium, while on screen their American friends wallowed in the mud with glazed eyes. And when the little bouncing balls came up onscreen, pointing out the sub-titled lyrics for 'Fixin' To Die Rag', the ciderheads were in seventh heaven. What was a night out without a sing-song? In broad Somerset accents they bellowed out the words, waving their flagons in unison. 'And it's one, two, three, what are we fighting for? Don't ask me I don't give a damn, next stop is Vietnam. And it's five, six, seven, open up the pearly gates. Ain't no time to wonder why, whoopee we're

On Saturdays in those Isle of Arran summers the picture palace became the dance hall. The splintery stage was then commanded by a gramophone roaring out 78 rpm hits of the period. Fronting it was a thin moustachioed man confined in a tight suit. With nothing but a pole up his back and a drum wedged between his legs he bashed away with panache, as if frantically sewing up a leaking willie with giant needle and thread.

(RON GEESIN)

all going to die!' Those who couldn't read the words made them up, and Tich, who'd lost his glasses, settled for singing 'Widecombe Fair' instead, coughing, spluttering and relishing his last night out.

(IAN BREAKWELL)

AN AFTERNOON AT THE OPERA

When I lived in Dublin at the end of the Second World War, one of my friends was an obsessive film buff whose dramatic recall, frame by frame, of scenes such as the Odessa Steps sequence from *Battleship Potemkin* or the final chase in Fritz Lang's *M* often hypnotized even the drunks in the bars we frequented. One afternoon we went together to see an Italian filmed opera in a small cinema off Grafton Street which specialised in foreign films. In his usual way, as soon as the film started, George began to give me a run down on the technical assets I might otherwise be missing. 'Observe, dear Lionel, the remarkable framing of the leg and its juxtaposition with the Corinthian column.' And so on. When, at the high point of the opera, *Norma*, the star began to get into her stride with '*Casta diva*', and George into his stride with gratuitous evaluations of the lighting and editing, a woman behind us brought a large bag of herrings smartly down on George's bald head, with the words: 'Will yer for Jesus's sake hold yer gob while I listen to that poor woman there!'

(LIONEL MISKIN)

SECOND EDIT

On an aeroplane you're helpless. The film you see is somebody else's choice, and it usually has George Segal in it. Once I watched a whole movie with the wrong soundtrack. It was *Fletch*, and when Chevy Chase spoke it was

Julie Andrews who came out of his mouth.

You're trapped in your headphones and trapped in your seat. You feel helpless, too, because you're watching it in danger. Cinemas are safe, that is one of their charms. They're dark and upholstered and warm as the womb. There's staff with uniforms to look after you. A plane cabin tries to fool you with the same set-up, but suddenly it meets turbulence, bumps and jolts, and three hundred of you sit there thinking of the drop beneath. In the middle of *A Man For All Seasons* there's a ping, and on come the little red signs: FASTEN YOUR SEATBELT. In front of the celluloid swordfight three hundred souls fear for their lives.

Once, coming back from New York, we were all watching a romantic comedy. It was interrupted by the captain's voice telling us that thanks to the strong following winds we would be arriving in London three quarters of an hour before schedule.

Trouble was, the film wasn't nearly finished. So a stewardess fast forwarded it. We sat, rigid in our seats, as chunks of gabbling plot sped by. Our suave heroes were transformed into Laurel and Hardy: suburban life speeded up into some manic, coronary inducing rush hour. How time flies! We were at our stewardess's mercy. She had promoted herself into the film's second editor, and slowed it down to normal at the bits she liked, and thought we would appreciate. These bits were the love scenes. Suddenly, once they were in each other's arms, our hero and heroine acted like normal human beings. According to our blonde stewardess, herself an object of fantasy, all life was a mindless rush, gabbled nonsense, sweaty commuting between the only moments that made sense, the embrace of a man and a woman. And how beautifully she stage managed it: as we touched down at Heathrow, the final credits were rolling.

(DEBORAH MOGGACH)

At this moment the creator of so many milestones in our young lives, our first childhood projections, lies somewhere in California, frozen stiff in a steel and glass drawer, boxed up well below zero. There Walt Disney awaits the kiss of cure, as if he were his own Sleeping Beauty.
(TONY JACKSON)

BLIND MAN'S MOVIE BUFF

The screen—the sail of the new voyages of discovery
Movies in flight—
the jet held on its course by the steady pressure of an image

Listen—the seeing eye dog
whines in the darkroom
Celluloid begins to yawn and flower

As the atomic submarine approaches the pole
the sailor beginning to crack leaps up in front of the
    projector

Across an outdoor cinema screen flaps a heavy un-
    identified bird

A berserk laundromatte—the last switches are being
    pulled in the control rooms of Atlantis T.V.

The montage gets too complex here—the film splits open
    with screams of laughter

The mad dentist is projecting
grand canyons into cavities
baby movies onto atom-clouds

The hands in the laps growing still
as the lava pours over Herculaneum

The hell within the negative—
throats nostrils and all orifices
glow with an unearthly inward burning

X-ray plates clenched between the teeth of skulls grinning
    on candid camera
snap into two—
And at last the darkroom door swings open

The seeing eye dog
is tracking the smell of burning
back to a cigarette on a luxury movie-house carpet
—Odour potent as the first
land-breeze

A field of crickets is heard distantly through the sound of
    the projector

We are drifting towards a mysterious landfall

The faint ground-flicker of interior universes
within the darkening screen.

(HARRY FAINLIGHT)

KETCHUP ARTISTES

A wet afternoon in Pwllheli. Lawrence of Arabia squinted across the dunes. He was wearing a tea towel all right, but Lawrence was a funny name for an Arab and he seemed confused about caravans. I suspected a con, especially when the shot horses didn't bleed.

The beach had been promised the night before, but rain had obliged an alternative treat. Going to the pictures fitted the bill: somewhere to go, something to do, a rarity shared by crowds of strangers. That week it was *Lawrence of Arabia*. Next week it was probably *The Sound of Music*. It usually was in Pwllheli, until the bingo.

I left the cinema with a rush of questions, mainly about blood, and a wise response answered them all: 'It's only a film.' The realisation dawned from that moment. Films were made up. They were trying to put one over on us and would no longer get away with it.

Puzzlement gave way to bravado and a new found delight in catching the ketchup artistes at it. Back home, matinees provided the chance to practise and shine. For a while it was enough to heckle the love scenes and cackle at disasters. When the novelty of criticism began to wear off we set up rival fringe performances. A bag of popcorn and a seat at the edge of the circle could attract more attention down below than *Flash Gordon*. A marble and a stalls back seat could be worth several minutes of noisy bagatelle. All this was kids' stuff though compared to the break into directing.

We were about ten when nuisance escalated into serious engagement. Someone pretty old told us moths flew to light. We already knew films were just projected light, as a spin-off discovery from experimentation with Park Drives.

Luckily, railway stations around Manchester kept their gas lamps well into the age of juvenile delinquency. The prospect of the moth scam was so exciting we even bought platform tickets so as not to blow it at the development stage. Captured moths were consigned to jamjars overnight to await the matinee.

The usherette was untrained in spotting sweaty palms. The film was unmemorable Elvis. Small guerrilla hands hovered ready to unscrew jamjar lids. The moths suffered a rousing shaking as the right moment was watched for. Framed by a swimming pool and women with pointed breasts, Elvis sneered lustily and was clearly about to burst into song. Off with the lids.

The exquisite timing would have been a credit to the deftest of film editors, but was wasted. The moths stayed

Painting by Ian Breakwell,
1988

put. Rattling the jars dislodged them. Three or four dropped into the darkness and choc ice wrappers, dead; a few fluttered aimlessly to rest around us; some took off into the vast space above.

Half the faces in the stalls were turned the wrong way, trying to see what the fuss was about in the back row. Anticipation turned to frustration. Recriminations flew. Too many privet leaves had made them dozy. Not enough holes in the lids had made them breathless.

Suddenly, they'd made it: huge black fluttering blots on the smooth features of a full frame Elvis. The cavalry had arrived, the dambusters had done it. Yells of triumph and foot stomping attracted the attention of the manager, who attracted ours with a long cane.

Thrown out, blinking, into the daylight, we wondered if they'd find the jars. If they did, would the silvery dust mean anything to them? Some of us wondered about the moths. We decided they'd be all right eating the bile yellow satin curtains. And we were famous anyway. The rest of the week was passed scrawling graffiti in splendid public places. Next Saturday we were frisked, just like in the films. The following week we took the Ritzy.

Like actors remembered as great for just turning up, the moths are recalled as gigantic, vivid images when they were probably just spectral smudges. They made a mark though.

(STEVE BUCKLEY)

> **The first night a girl put her hand inside my trousers was during a Kenneth More film about the sinking of the *Titanic*. It was called *A Night to Remember*.**
>
> (MIKE EVANS)

NILE ON FIRE

As we enter the darkened cinema it is around 11.30 p.m. and the seats are quickly filling with various rowdies, late-night drinkers and revellers to whom we eagerly add ourselves. In the cinema foyer the two old ladies who run the cinema are both dispensing and receiving abuse from all sides as to the quality of the night's offerings, *Storm Over the Nile* and *Voodoo Woman*. They are dressed in blue nylon housecoats over knee length silver boots.

As we sit down to enjoy the show the lights dim and the inevitable Pearl & Dean advertising slot comes hurtling out of the screen. Immediately we realise that something is very wrong. The sound has been increased to such a volume that, as I turn my head as if from a physical blow, I notice rows of heads with their eyes staring wildly and hair blown back as in a fierce gale. I stumble up the aisle to the immense ponderous tones of a god extolling the virtues of a restaurant in Moscow Road, Bayswater, and pass through some dingy curtains into the foyer. I try to explain to the two silver boots (now accompanied by the projectionist, drinking tea) what is wrong but I cannot make myself heard even out here. By pointing to my ears and making signs I eventually elicit the response from the projectionist, 'I'll turn it down when I've had my tea.'

During the first film, *Storm Over the Nile*, there is such a storm of noise in the cinema from the drunken audience that it proves impossible to follow the plot at all. After about an hour when the pies and chips have stopped flying across the screen I notice a strange purple growth, like a cancer cell under a microscope, at the bottom left hand corner of the screen. Growing in the most sinister manner, it is embedded in a battle scene taking place across the River Nile. Suddenly at the height of the battle this purple and now orange mushroom bursts across the entire screen, devouring both armies in its path.

Immediately and without any explanation the screen darkens and the deafening strains of 'Bye Bye Blackbird' burst from the speakers.

(NICK CUDWORTH)

A double bill in the afternoon. I sit next to a down and out who has salvaged his lunch from the bins. He reaches into his bag, brings out a sandwich, then stands up and inspects it in the projector beam to see what it contains. He has a classic sense of gastronomic order. Meat and cheese must come after fish; there is fruit for dessert. The whole meal takes almost an hour and makes me ravenous.

(PETE AYRTON)

LE CINEMA AU PEUPLE!

A film festival in one of the poorest countries in the world, Burkina Faso, celebrating the development of authentic, indigenous African cinema. Last night a group of small children sang 'L'Internationale', uncertain about the words, out of tune, but with an authenticity and optimism that is no longer possible in Europe.

La Patrie ou mort nous vaincrons![1] Here, this evening, in a local open air cinema on the sprawling outskirts of a one storey town (Secteur 14), the screening of a political documentary from Ghana with a Radio Moscow soundtrack. The commentary is largely ignored by an animated audience that talks while watching and participates by applauding the rich images of trays of ripe fruit and tomatoes in the marketplace in Managua, Nicaragua. Then Comrade President Thomas Sankara stepping off a plane, during a state visit, inspects a row of soldiers and salutes a flag.

*Street scene, Burkina Faso
(photo: Rod Stoneman)*

L'Ecran africain aux films africains![2] The noises of scuttling and rustling on the concrete floor. Glancing down to see brown rats moving confidently amongst the metal chairlegs, sniffling at the discarded sweet papers and orange peel. The audience is blithely unconcerned as the rats' rancid pink tongues stretch out to lick gently at pink heels.

(ROD STONEMAN)

[1] The Motherland or Death—we will win!
[2] The African screen for African films!

MOMA

The film shows at the Museum of Modern Art attract a strange audience. Very old people who come to all the shows tend to talk throughout the experimental work or leave. People drift in and out. The serious remain. Very big audiences become small ones. It's a hard crowd to figure.

One night I was there, before the start of the film, a young man leaped onto the stage and announced that he was an unemployed actor looking for a role in a movie. He pointed to his seat and urged anyone interested to contact him then and there. Smiling he leaped from the stage and the audience applauded. We became a more relaxed crowd and I remarked casually to the elderly woman beside me, 'New York's such a crazy place.'

Her answer was less casual. She replied: 'Yes, that's because of the Galiciani. The Litvaks are *not* funny.' She paused and continued: 'The English are Jews. Gaelic is Hebrew but no one knew this until Pitman invented shorthand and then without the vowels it was clear that Gaelic and Hebrew were the same. The English *are* Jews.' Her hand waved in front of her and she said: 'My daughter wrote the best art book ever written. It's across the street in the Donnell Library. My husband invented radar. All the books are across the street.' I consider this as the lights dim.

(LYNNE TILLMAN)

STRANGLING IN THE STALLS

Festival crowds here in Montreal are a committed lot. By the time the two week World Film Festival winds down at the beginning of September most of the cinephiles standing in the long queues at the box office have no idea what they're waiting for; they'll watch anything that moves. Once in the cinema, openness of mind and concentration tend to be their trademarks. So it was with some surprise a few years ago that our attention was drawn from the dull French *film noir* onscreen to the back of the cinema, where a couple were resolving a lovers' squabble. The man had his fingers around the woman's throat and was banging her head against the back of the seat. When another patron tried to step in, the enraged lover flew at him. An usher made an unsuccessful attempt to separate the two men, but it took the intervention of the woman to calm things down. She guided her emotional mate back to his seat and sat with her arms around him until he tried to kill her again. This scene was repeated at five minute intervals until the police arrived.

(BARBARA SAMUELS)

CINEPHILES

The National Film Theatre in London shows a wonderful variety of films but obviously has little of the atmosphere of the high street picture palace. Even the bars and foyers are reminiscent of nothing so much as an airport lounge, an impression reinforced by the tannoy announcements of five, three and one minute calls for *Casablanca, Paris Texas* and *Roma*. But strange people, outcasts from public cinemas, can become members of the National Film Theatre by anonymous postal application. So the stodgy respectability of the official state cinema becomes leavened with curious characters. The tweedy lady, very county, who suffered from some extreme fungoid disease of her feet, which were wrapped in many layers of polythene and which in a public cinema would have guaranteed her a whole row to herself, but at the NFT caused whoever was unfortunate to have the adjoining numbered seat to retain vivid Aromavision memories of particular films. Colonel Flasher, very military bearing, exposed himself with parade ground precision. Napoleon's Number One Fan, who during Abel Gance's film was accused by the man in the next seat of masturbating underneath his hat and splashing his wife, but who stoutly defended himself by saying that the unfortunate staining would never have happened if she hadn't nudged him and thus dislodged the titfer from his lap.

And then there was Our Lady of the Leftovers who entered the NFT bar wearing a fur stole and carrying a sequinned evening bag. Her face lit up with a delighted smile as she gazed at an abandoned plate of half-eaten sandwiches on a nearby table. She stuffed the sandwiches into her evening bag and continued on her way, her eyes sparkling.

With special affection I remember the metro railway enthusiasts who, confronted by rigorous structuralist films or scenes of sexual and scatalogical excess, walked out of the cinema in baffled confusion during the first NFT International Underground Film Festival and indignantly demanded their money back after having booked for a whole season of what seemed like fascinating specialist

In the first scene of *Annie Hall* Woody Allen was talking directly at the audience. The man behind me leant forward and whispered in my ear, 'Tell that guy to quit yapping will you? Tell him I wanna watch this film.'
(TIMOTHY EMLYN JONES)

The manager was patrolling the aisles and found a pair of lady's panties on the floor by the back stalls. He picked them up and courteously enquired of the young woman sitting closest with her boyfriend if they were hers. With equal decorum she replied, 'Oh no, mine are in my handbag.'

(NOEL SPENCE)

delights: German Underground, American Underground, Italian Underground.

Meanwhile, back in the 'bar area' the deadly serious cinephiles for whom going to the cinema had as much magic as attending evening class droned endlessly on. An elegantly dressed man and an elegantly dressed woman were sitting opposite each other. She was dressed in a two-piece suit, the skirt just above her knees, and black calf-length boots. He was dressed in casual wear: grey sweater and slacks with knife edge creases. He was telling her who, in his opinion, are the most important French film directors, pausing only to adjust the creases in his trousers. She listened, her little finger cocked as she held her coffee cup poised above its saucer. As he spoke he broke the seal on the carton of cream for his coffee, inadvertently squeezed the carton, and squirted a little jet of cream up her skirt between her thighs.

(IAN BREAKWELL)

BROBDINGNAG

I don't know how it came to be shown at the Carlton, East Ham, but one Sunday my parents took me to see *The Sheep Has Five Legs* starring the French comedian Fernandel. I was nine years old and this was the first foreign film I'd seen (probably the first most people had seen in East London). As far as I recall Fernandel played all five brothers in five linked episodes. The part I vividly remember was about a South Seas tramp steamer captain. The scene was set in a cabin on the boat with two men (one Fernandel) and a beautiful Tahitian girl wearing only a grass skirt. In front of each man on the table was a lump of sugar and sealed in the cabin with them was a fly. If the fly landed on your sugar lump you got the girl. The tension mounted as the fly buzzed round the room giving the audience, every now and again, a fleeting glimpse of the girl. I was already sliding down in my seat trying to indicate to my parents without actually looking away from the screen that I wasn't at all interested, when suddenly there was a close shot of the fly as it settled on her shoulder. The camera followed it down as it walked across her breast (thirty foot wide) and past her nipple (five foot high). What a sight! I sank down further until I could just see over the seat in front. What a Sunday afternoon!

(JOHN CHRISTIE)

THE OPAQUE SCREEN

When I was six my grandparents took me to see a film which I was told to observe closely because I would learn lessons about good behaviour and deportment from one of the juvenile characters. All I remember is that at one point he walked along with one foot on the kerb and the other in the gutter and was told off for limping. After the film I tried it myself, with similar results.

Since then I have always had trouble with films that were supposed to teach me something, or from which I hoped to learn. Film shows at school on the manufacture of coal gas intercut interesting views of hot coke being extruded from retorts with dull shots of gas scrubbers removing sulphur compounds from the hot gas. But neither at school nor at home was there a gas supply. I knew that occasionally people put their heads in gas ovens, but there was no mention of that.

When I looked to films for information on sexual and romantic matters they were not much help either. It seemed that in emotional encounters men and women stood face to face, talking excited nonsense while each looked with agitation into their partner's eyes. Then, unless gangsters broke in and disturbed them, they lay down and the screen went hazy, then the lights went out. Slide shows were just as bad. I went to a lecture on hermaphroditism. The introduction was all about X and Y chromosomes in embryology, and I fell asleep. I woke to see through half open eyes enormous Technicolour images of baffling genitalia filling the wall. To this day just to see or

I was watching *Stalag 17* with my grandmother and being felt up by a dirty old man. I was disconcerted but the fascination with the film went on. I was seven years old. It was an almost empty theatre in Long Beach, Long Island, a tourist spot with a boardwalk and beautiful beaches. I came out and told granny, she was ashamed of me. We never went there again.

(SUZANNAH HALL)

hear the word 'hermaphrodite' is sufficient to make those luminous pictures shimmer before my eyes.

The seeds of further sexual confusion were sown by the custom, in the cinemas of Wellington, Shropshire, where I lived, of spraying the audience with perfumed deodorant during the intervals. Sometimes I smell that odour as a perfume on women, like sweet Harpic.

Then came military service and a training film on snipers. Two men with muddied faces and bracken on their helmets are in a ruined building, trying to spot an enemy rifleman. At an upstairs window they present a life size dummy head: firm jaw, aquiline nose, shining complexion. Crack! The head disappears backwards. Aha, just as they thought, and they have kept a lookout for movement, a flash that reveals the enemy position. But questions remain as the film continues. Do soldiers really carry around realistic papier-mâché heads just in case? If, having signed for one of these heads, they return it with the nose shot off, what then? Did some firm have a contract to produce these heads, and in what quantities: a hundred, a gross, a thousand? Is there somewhere an MOD store, perhaps underground at Box Hill, a long wooden building smelling of oil and blankets, with row upon row of heads, snipers for the use of, gathering dust while the rosy, hand tinted complexions fade to chalk and grey plaster? Code name 'Warhead'?

(P P O'LEARY)

THE HEN THAT LAID THE SILVER EGG

At the end of the war my neighbour Mrs Cooper was young Giovanna Boccalon, growing up in Pasiano, an Italian village not far from Treviso. Those were lean years, without money for trips to the cinema. But the Boccalons kept chickens.

Giovanna and her friend Ninetta were willing to help with the hens, in fact to provide physical assistance in the premature delivery of eggs. While Giovanna sang en-

'With one bound he was free.' And we were too.
(JOHN CONQUEST)

couragingly, stroked and patted the chicken's back, Ninetta watched underneath for any result. Patience was essential.

On a good day, eggs in their pockets, they would set off knowing the silver screen was theirs. The cinema was tiny, run single-handed by Neno Rossi, who would store the entrance eggs in straw and then run the projector. By the time films reached Pasiano they were far from pristine: they might be unintentionally silent and sometimes stopped altogether. Giovanna would return home, ravished but resentful. To her criticisms her mother would say: 'Well, what do you expect for an egg?'

(MAGGI HAMBLING)

Kids and chicks, Easter matinee at the Stepney Troxy, 1950s

FADING EDDIE

Each year, shortly before graduation, the sixth grade class of my elementary school was treated to a day of sun, roller skating, hot-dog gorging and swimming pool frolics at Jones Beach, Long Island. The day came, and with it a forty days, forty nights style rainstorm. We felt damned. I'm sure none of us noticed what must have been expressions of pure panic on the faces of our two teachers and the several parents who had volunteered to keep their own children and their classmates from certain death by drowning in the pool. But some desperate quick thinker had phoned Radio City Music Hall, that palace of film, live shows and the mighty Wurlitzer. This was long before 'X' or any other ratings except those of the Catholic Church, and no one thought or cared to ask what was playing. We arrived, toting our towels, watched the Radio City Music Hall Rockettes do their synchronised high kicks (a great bunch those Rockettes), the curtains parted in front of the screen, the symbol of the film studio appeared (I've always loved this part, but was it a lady or a lion?), and the title of the film zoomed forward: *The Eddie Duchin Story*, starring Tyrone Power, my mother's favourite. The film ended as poor Eddie met his Maker in a way unmemorable except in visual

In the sleeper compartment of a train speeding through the night a youth crouches over a naked woman he has drugged with a hypodermic syringe. The youth unwraps a razor blade and slices through the veins of her wrist, fastening his lips to the wound as he hungrily drinks the spurting blood. The man in the row in front arches backwards over his seat, his breath sucked in through clenched teeth.

(IAN BREAKWELL)

terms: he sat at his piano becoming lighter and lighter in tone. I found myself thinking, 'Old piano players never die, they just fade away.' I think this was my first conscious experience of cynicism in response to sentimentality.

(ELENA ALEXANDER)

TRICK

There are a couple of sequences in *The Gaucho* that stay etched in the memory. In one Douglas Fairbanks tells a woman to follow him and when faced with her persistent refusal, arguing as she does that she cannot abandon her home, he tethers his horses to the latter and carts the whole house off in a burst of white-toothed laughter. At another moment in the film a door is closed and we see a key in the lock. The gaucho slips a rug under the door, ejects the key and then recovers it by hauling the rug towards him. As simple as can be, except that nowhere in the world have I encountered a door with such a gap between it and the floor. Thirty-five years later I saw the film again in New York. But the time to 'recognise' it image by image had gone; just as the moments of each day fade away, so I'd forgotten it.

A more precise impression remains of *Shoulder Arms*, seen around the same time. It concerns the famous sequence in the flooded trench when the soldiers are getting ready to spend the night. Charlie Chaplin lies down, his body disappears from view, then his head.

Even today I remember my stupefaction close to terror. Because I couldn't countenance how you could stay under water without being asphyxiated, and yet at the same time I was incapable of comprehending the trick. Faced with a fact that was visually undeniable I was snared in the total impossibility of 'understanding' it. In short, here was an extremely succinct initiation into the notion of the 'existence' of the world, once religious fakery had been eliminated.

(MARCEL MARIËN)

WATER AND DREAMS

I fell into a swimming pool. My mother found me floating face downwards and I was saved by artificial respiration. After that I had a fear of water, especially the sea, but I learned to live with it and even became a good swimmer. Then, when I was grown up I saw the film *The Sinking of the Titanic* and it brought back the terror. People were floundering in the water. My nightmares returned at a time when everything was crowding in on me and I couldn't cope. I decided to commit suicide, by drowning. I made two attempts but they both failed, each time my fear of water proved too much. The first time I went back to a lake where I used to go as a child. I tried to knock myself out with some cider I'd bought, then I swallowed a bottle of weedkiller and started to walk towards the lake. But I'd bought the wrong weedkiller, it was Tumbleweed and I found out later it's only lethal to tropical fish, apparently I should have bought Pathklear which is much stronger. I was suddenly violently sick and fell into a ditch. When I came round I felt much better and I turned my back on the lake and went home. The second time I caught a bus to the coast. The brambles were head high, my face got all scratched. Eventually I reached the cliff top. Down below were lots of fishing boats

I walked into the college cinema to find the tutor watching the film on his own. 'This fucking audience is getting me down,' he said. 'It hasn't turned up again!'

(TIMOTHY EMLYN JONES)

and I decided to wait until they returned to the harbour. I lay down across the path. Some time later a man came along the path and stopped to ask me if I was all right, I told him yes and to please go away, which he did but I thought he'll go to fetch help so I'd better do it now. I took off my rings and jewellery and put them in my handbag then lowered myself over the cliff edge. I slid down until I became entangled in some bracken. I looked down at the sea breaking on the rocks. I became paralysed, unable to go down or up. Then I heard voices saying, 'Is this where she was? Here's her bag. She's down the cliff.' They must have rescued me, I can't remember anything except my terror of the dark sea.

I don't think I would ever do such a thing again, but when the depression settles on me I'm very vulnerable, and if I went to see a film and it had a drowning sequence in it, or swirling water, then you just can't tell. People say it's only a film but they don't know.

(LISA MONTAGUE)

BLUE WATER

A John Wayne film. A fight spills out of a saloon. A cowboy falls into the horse trough, which is full of bright blue water. Then he is repeatedly dunked in it. What I remember is the unrealistic blueness of the water. I had never seen water that was *that* blue.

Thirty years on I saw it again, when I started going to the Aegean. Most days there was that colour spread from the shore to the sky, bigger than a horse trough.

One summer I stayed in Molyvos on Lésvos. They have an open-air cinema there. A toilet with a hose to wash it down, a kiosk from which to sell tickets and Pepsi-Cola, and a rude shelter for a projector they never secure. And a wall. You sit on rows of stacking chairs. Intermittently a film is projected at the wall. All kinds of films. Films with women with big breasts and cars and fighting. Cars got the biggest response. The most forceful shout was for a Toyota truck on a stand in a showroom. It was big and it gleamed. It was in the film to be blown apart. And there was a man handcuffed to his chair. In his other hand a grenade with the pin removed so he couldn't put it down to free himself from the handcuffs, and so from the chair, and so from the room. Lots of explosions in that film. Lots of advice from the audience: gasps, sighs of sympathy, roars of contempt, screams.

Coke cans, once emptied, would arc over the heads of the audience. Good throwers could hit Lee Marvin or Clint Eastwood full in the face. And always the unawareness of the actors that anything had touched them: not a flinch. The cans banged and rattled over a fuzzy soundtrack already overlaid with calls to Vassilis to move his head or Kostas to provide a cigarette.

Out of the darkness beyond the white wall, streaks of fireflies: sudden lines of light matching the projected gashes on the film, which would suddenly stop and the lights come up to make an interval. Often elements of the story would be edited out by the interval. If the projectionist didn't like the film it didn't get shown, or only part of it. Sometimes events were shown reordered or shown twice. Sometimes no picture for a while. Sometimes no sound. They sold many Pepsi-Colas.

One night along came *Doctor Strangelove*, so we went out early to eat before the film started, in a taverna near the cinema. We chose something quick to prepare. And they took a long time making it. And they took a long time serving it. And while they were taking their time we argued about something else. Some small argument, but it was immobilising. As we sat there *Doctor Strangelove* began. We listened to the soundtrack through the back wall of the cinema, separated from each other by plates filmed in olive oil with pools of tomato juice, and half finished wine. Alcohol and heat, unreason against unreason. And the aural projection of a film mocking unreason, mocking stupidity.

Two years later: Batsi, on the island of Andros. Another open-air cinema. The same communality, the same responses. We were watching a film with many trees in it. It began to rain. In the film. It began to rain. In Greece. In the

When we were twelve our aspiring sex lives were chronicled by seat location in the cinema. If you sat with a girl in rows A to F, you'd just met. F to M you were undoubtedly snogging (mouths closed). M to P was snogging (mouths open). While P to V meant access to the inside of a liberty bodice. I never could believe what they said happened in rows behind V.

(CHRIS PROCTOR)

One night in 1962 Kurdish rebels entered a Kirkuk cinema disguised as policemen and silently surrounded an officer known to be torturing opponents of the government. They took him outside and up into the mountains. Then they threw him over a precipice.

(SALAH FAIQ)

world outside of the film. In our world. We sat in the rain, looking at filmed rain. Some of the audience calmly fetched additional chairs from a store and we each sat holding our stacking chair over our heads until the shower subsided, in about the same time it took the film rain to subside.

We walked home in the dark along the wet road around the bay. Car headlights made it difficult to see, in the way that an usherette's torch can temporarily blind. On our right the dark sea which, if the sun were back on, would have been an impossible blue.

(LAWRENCE UPTON)

DRIVE-IN

The perfect evening would be sometime in August when the heat of the summer is distilled and concentrated and the ground in the pine forests has become brown and crackly, the tarmac on the roads quite soft. At eight o'clock I get into my car, a Chevy with bench seats in the front and the back, no bucket seats. I drive down the strip past the car dealerships and the drive-in motels with their dusty swimming pools out front. I stop at the drive-in bank then I drive out the highway to the lake to pick up my date. We

have a quick swim in the dark, cold water, touching the sandy bottom with our toes as we dive off the raft, the evening still bright, still hot. Then we drive down to the drive-in restaurant where we eat lots of crap including a double order of onion rings.

About 10.00, dusk, we motor over to the drive-in which is showing a triple bill of horror movies. We park near the back of the lot. My date gets out of the car to go buy popcorn while I fix up the speaker. When my date comes back the credits are rolling on the first film. We settle in to watch.

All of the films are about teenagers getting massacred by monsters. The first to die are always the ones who have had sex with each other. The heroes and heroines are nearly always virgins. This makes my date and me laugh. There is a lot to do in a dark car late at night besides staring across the roofs of other parked cars at flickering images on a screen. We turn off the speaker.

(KATE PULLINGER)

IN THE FLESH

In 1970 I was a member of an Anglo-American theatre troupe, the Wherehouse La Mama Company. One afternoon Beth Porter, an American founder member of the company, invited the rest of us to a double bill of soft core porno movies in Piccadilly. Eight of us took our places in the small but crowded cinema. Some of us, including Beth, sat in the front row. Our four female members were the only women in the audience. The reason for our excursion was that, back in the USA, Beth had taken a leading role in one of the films now showing. Being a radical experimental company of the time, given to onstage nudity, we were no strangers to Beth's voluptuous physique and it was hard to suppress our giggles at the absurd movie, in which a deformed, slobbering handyman ogles and gropes our heroine before coming to a violent end. But our real kick came at the end of the film when the lights went up. Beth

Surrounded by local hardknocks, Bob Golden was the only gringo in a Taos, New Mexico, fleapit. The film was a western, and the moment John Wayne walked onscreen a rain of knives traversed the auditorium and killed his image.

(PAUL HAMMOND)

rose from her front row seat, turned, and allowed the audience to get a good look at her before making her way out. A frisson of disbelief and unease passed though the male patrons as the woman they had been watching in simulated copulation on the screen materialised in the flesh before their very eyes.

(NEIL HORNICK)

YMIR AT THE COLISEUM

The Coliseum in Green Lanes, North London, was originally a Victorian music hall. Refitted as a cinema in the early years of this century it subsequently became a bingo hall and finally a flood-damaged carpet warehouse. In the early 1960s one result of shrinking cinema audiences was the Sunday double bill of low budget horror movies. One of these was a 1957 black and white feature called *20,000,000 Miles to Earth*, in which a spaceship, returning from Venus, crashes into the sea. A canister is recovered from the craft, the contents of which solidify into an at first small creature called an Ymir. The creature grows at an alarming rate, then escapes and cuts a swathe of destruction as it moves through the southern Italian countryside. It approaches Rome, lumbering up the Appian Way, doubling its size every few minutes. The pursuing army patrol the streets in jeeps with mounted machine guns, until one soldier flings his arm into the air, pointing: 'Look,' he shouts 'there it is on top of the Colosseum!' At this, a girl in the audience with a beehive hair-do leaps to her feet screaming, 'Where? Where?' Others in the auditorium begin whistling and stamping their feet. There is a rush for the door, the audience spill out into the road, stopping the traffic and gesturing wildly at the roof of the cinema.

(TERRY GENIN)

When the shapeless *Blob* cornered the heroine Tina, a voice came from the back of the stalls, 'You're all right Tina, he's got no thingy.'

(MIKE EVANS)

Buster Keaton leaves the projection box to enter the movie itself

THE RUSH

On Mickey Colbeck's birthday his mother invited us to a lunchtime party at their house. This was to be followed by a free trip to the Plaza. Excitedly, the pack of noisy urchins devoured potted meat butties and wolfed dribbling jam tarts swilled down with Ben Shaw's dandelion and burdock pop. If I remember exactly, the gathering included Hilton Whitwam, his sister Pauline, Roger Hanson, Christine Downs and Michael Colbeck's brother, Trevor. And me of course. The presents were opened and Mr Colbeck scraped out a discordant 'Happy Birthday to You' on his cheap violin with a yowling rejoinder from the assembled rag, tag and bobtail brigade of youngsters. After the candles on the cake had been blown out, each of us was given a slice which was wrapped in a serviette. We also got a tanner each to buy goodies on our arrival at the Plaza. After searching for ages, Roger Hansons' cap, which had slipped down the back of the sideboard, was found and the noisy pack hurried down the road to catch the trolley bus to the centre of the universe, the Plaza.

Mrs Colbeck had a difficult time keeping the unruly pack in order on the bus. She wasn't a well woman. For years she had suffered from Parkinson's disease, and on many occasions Michael had been reduced to tears by the tauntings of the other kids in the schoolyard who mimicked his mother's ditherings and shakings. Her condition wasn't improved by the fact that she constantly sucked Rennies, which left a white residue around her mouth. Although they were a poor family, her kindness came to the fore at such events and her savings were decimated to make the party memorable. She wore a coat that had seen better days. Around her hair she wore a length of Petersham ribbon. Arnold her husband, also ailing, worked every hour God sent at the local fireworks factory. He reminded me of Stan Laurel.

The bus arrived at the Plaza and we were all checked, the boys to see if their hair was straight and the girls for hair ribbon adjustment. Our clothes were scrutinised too. After all they were our Sunday best. Then on to the queue and the jibes of the other kids about coming to the cinema with an adult. They soon shut up after we proudly announced that we were being paid for and had a whole tanner each to spend.

We entered the foyer and Mrs Colbeck bought the tickets. We watched the machine dispensing a long string of orange receipts. Then, as one, we shot to the kiosk to buy refreshments with our tanners. The war ration existed for some years after the war itself and things were scarce. We greedily surveyed the packets of Spangles, popcorn and cheap orange drinks that were neatly displayed behind the glass. Ice cream was on sale too. After we had each made a selection, we went to the entrance of the auditorium.

Standing at the doorway was a man in a shabby suit. He took the tickets from Mrs Colbeck, tore them in half and threaded the ends onto a spike that hung from the wall beside him. He put on a plastic smile and said, 'Tha's gotten thi work cut out fo' thi this afternoo'in Missis.'

'Well it's our Michael's birthday an' yuv got to gi''em a bit of summat ampt ya?' she retorted.

'Better thee th' me,' sneered the man. He scowlingly eyed Michael for some minor offence he had committed in previous weeks. Michael pleadingly eyed the man back as if to say, 'Please don't tell mi mum or she'll kill me.' The man glowered and muttered, 'It's a good job it's ya birthday or bloomin' otherwise...' Fortunately his mother was out of earshot or it would have been 'otherwise', birthday or not.

Once in the cinema itself, we were shown to our seats by a woman who doubled as ice cream lady and usherette. Her skeletal form was draped with an oversize overall that had been laundered so many times that the embroidered 'PLAZA' on the top pocket had faded. She had a big mole on her top lip from which a couple of long ginger hairs coiled. Her hair was rolled up around the edges like a continuous sausage. It was all held together by a million hair grips. As she walked ahead of us to show us our seats, she wiggled and stumbled trying to stay upright in her high heels which were a size too big. Once in our seats a cackle of voices chattered: 'I can't see'; 'Don't eat 'em all now or you'll 'ave none for later'; 'Shurrup or I'll bash yer up'; and 'My dad's bigger'n yours and he'll bash his brains out.' Above all this crackling speakers, dotted around the auditorium, played a popular tune by a dance band with a crooner sliding from one note to another: 'Wh-e-y-an tha-a bb-blue u-o-orrv a-tha na-ight mey-eets tha-a-go-ow-ld orr-v tha da-ii-y.'

Suddenly, as if by magic, the place went silent. The only sound to be heard was the scraping of an ancient dimmer board bringing the lights down. More music then the clattering of the silken flounces of the curtain rising ceilingwards and gathering in great bulbous lumps under the pelmet of the proscenium. The stage lamps faded and then total darkness. The screen flashed with blobs of speckled light. This was accompanied by lots of bottom shufflings in the audience whose voices were now coming back into action: 'Shush' and 'Shurrup, it's starting'. It was time for the adverts, still projections claiming the merits of Farm Stores Gold Medal Pork Pies, Ivy Coaches, Rita's High Class Hairdressers, Dentons Garage for reliable repairs, Stringers for burst pipes, Shop at the Co-op.

These finished and the films started proper. Numbers flickered onto the screen in rapid progression and the fanfare of a Merry Melodies cartoon swiped the open mouthed audience into Woody Woodpecker or the Road Runner. Astoundment changed to laughter and laughter to cheering as the characters hurtled into million foot deep

The price of patriotism: in a letter to the the local paper Mr R W Watson wrote, 'Last night I stood for the playing of the National Anthem in a Glasgow suburban cinema and when I got to the door I found I'd been locked in.'

I saw five films during one night, one after the other, finishing with *Woman of the Dunes*, a print in the original Japanese with Czech subtitles. In a peculiar state, almost asleep, I heard the whole thing in English.

(TOM RAWORTH)

Abandoned projection box,
Queens Cinema,
Thornaby-on-Tees (photo:
Derek Smith)

canyons, and sticks of dynamite blew the hair off cats. Next came the latest episode of *Flash Gordon and the Claymen*. The spaceships and rayguns crackled and growled. Kids cowered behind their seats as the terrifying Ming ordered his palace guard to carry out some ghastly deed. Nobody worried about the join in the pointy receding hairline of Ming's brow or the bits of string that held the looming spaceships in front of the sparkling cardboard galaxy.

Hilton Whitwam, being a little shorter than the rest of us, couldn't see and Mrs Colbeck leaned over and told him to sit on the back of his seat. It gave him a better vantage point but in turn deprived an irate youngster behind him of his view. After much squeaking of seats, grumblings and shouts, the problem was resolved and now the party resumed its enjoyment. Suddenly the Flash Gordon episode came to a close with someone about to be crushed to death. 'To Be Continued' filled the screen and immediately the whole cinema burst into their own version of what the outcome would be: 'There's a secret panel'; 'I bet he's got a raygun hidden up his jumper' and so on.

Hopalong Cassidy was the next film. Roger Hanson, who suffered from a stammer, bounced around in his seat powing verbal sixguns throughout. The lights then went up and it was the interval and the ice cream woman. Scratchy music accompanied an almost invisible film advertising the wares of the lady who stood, not quite centre, in a spotlight at the side of the stage. Some of the kids, unable to wait until she came up the aisle, shot to the front of the house for theirs. When eventually she came up to our part of the cinema, Mrs Colbeck bought us each an ice cream. It was Collettas in a brick wrapped in paper. We gobbled them, chins were wiped and the lights went down again.

'Mrs Colbeck,' moaned an urgent Christine Downs, 'I want to go for a wee wee.' 'Oh 'eck, come on then, 'urry up,' replied Mrs Colbeck, looking at the girl's legs which were so crossed that if she folded them anymore they wouldn't have been able to be undone. She was unceremoniously bundled through the door marked 'Ladies' at the front of the cinema. As they returned, Christine in her haste ran up the aisle so as not to miss the film which had already started.

On the line 'And a Babycham for my baby' Martin decided to take a leak. Drunk, disorderly, barely able to contain himself, he bounded up the stairs, undoing his flies as he went. Bursting through a door, cock in hand, he found himself in the projection box. The room was empty. 'It was like discovering the *Marie Celeste*, everything in order, but nobody around.' Afterwards an almost relieved man located the Gents.
(LES COLEMAN)

She didn't notice the skinny ice cream lady who was walking backwards down the aisle. Her head collided with the ice cream woman's stomach and almost unsaddled her from her high heels. Mrs Colbeck proffered an apologetic 'Kids', and started along the row to her seat. This set off a gang of youngsters in the back rows who started shouting in mock protest, 'Sit down, Missus, we can't see for your bum.' Yells of laughter ensued and then a competition as the young wits of the valley tried to outdo one another, blew raspberries, belched and then someone managed a real fart which brought the house down. Mrs Colbeck reprimanded our group as we roared in tearful laughter. From behind us came another voice. It was the man with the striped suit giving the offender a good ticking off.

'You'll either shut up or a'll ah thi out. And thee, none of thi owd book. Don't think ah don't know thi father. E'll 'ear o' this then it'll be tears'. Silence reigned again except for the sound of the jungle. Tarzan was swinging through the trees. Jane was in the tree house cooking and Boy was playing some daft game with Cheetah on the ground below. Meanwhile the baddies were hacking their way through the jungle, intent on nicking the diamonds from the Umbo Jumbo tribe. It was at the point of an elephant stampede (Indian elephants with lumps of tarpaulin on their ears to make them look like African ones) that a different drama was beginning to take place.

Mrs Colbeck looked towards her Michael and realised that his eyes were closed. She nudged him. She shook him. No response. She jumped to her feet, pushed along the row and ran up the aisle to the rear of the cinema. 'It's our Michael. I think e's ailin',' came her distressed voice in the darkness. ' 'ang on a minute can yer, Missus,' the voice of stripe suit echoed. A glimmer of light flashed from the rear of the cinema and the man ran out into the foyer. The pair of them came back to the seats and pushed the kids out of the way to get to the slumping Michael. Stripe suit was carrying a pint pot, brim full of water that splashed on the line of kids as they pushed past. 'Our Michael, our Michael,' the woman said in despair, 'I think e's dead. Oo 'e's dead. Ah know 'e's dead.' She snatched the water from stripe suit's hand and without further ado chucked it into the boy's

Led by the feeble beam of the usherette's torch I proceed behind my mother, terrified and disoriented, along what I presume is the top of a precipice to our cliff top seats, with only the screen far below breaking the darkness. Throughout the film I try to make sense of the vertiginous black abyss around us. When the lights come up all is revealed.

(DAVID BRIERS)

face. The three rows behind got their share of it too. A coughing spluttering boy awoke from his own private movie. He'd been in a deep sleep. 'Dozy bitch,' snapped stripe suit. 'I mean't for 'im to sup it not for it to be keffed all 'ort pictures.'

Tarzan got his man, we had our treat and stripe suit got a severe reprimand from Mrs Colbeck. ''Ow dare you talk ter me like that, ya jumped up little 'itler,' she blurted, spraying the quaking stripe suit with Rennie spit.

I look back on those Saturdays sometimes and I can't watch an old Tarzan film on TV without remembering old stripe suit copping the sharp end of Mrs Colbeck's tongue. Sadly, Mrs Colbeck died from her Parkinson's disease. Her husband, Arnold, is dead too, as is Michael's brother Trevor. I suppose stripe suit is sat sulking somewhere, hating life, people and especially flipping kids.

(IAN HINCHLIFFE)

SUMMERTIME

Toward the end of July the sidewalks in New York City heat up, the subways turn to steambaths, and an afternoon becomes something to be avoided; so many people go to the revival houses that they do their best business in the summertime. There's a comforting familiarity to a second or third viewing, but the real reason I sit in the dark at high noon is the thrill of sweat evaporating on the back of my neck and that first shiver that makes me wish I had brought a sweater when just minutes before the thought of wool would have been masochistic.

Badlands is a cult favourite around town and the theatre was packed that afternoon. Sitting up front is always my first choice, but in the summertime I need an aisle. There are a lot of bare arms in a theatre in summertime. I took the aisle seat three rows from the back.

Generally there's little conversation in the theatre before the show starts because a lot of people go to revival houses by themselves. Many bring books to read until the

I'd walked around Paris for days, looking for a room. Then in bright yellow letters above a cinema I saw *Chambre à Louer* (Room to Let), pasted diagonally across a poster. A room over a cinema, very French, perfect. I went in. 'It's about the room,' I said to the woman in the kiosk.

(JUDY KRAVIS)

lights go down. Some display titles prominently on their laps as an intellectual come-on: 'Talk to me, I'm literate.' I play the stereotype game.

A young woman across the aisle from me was not reading *Death, Sleep, and the Traveller*. She chewed her popcorn like she was afraid to make noise. I decided she was an English grad student who sees a psychiatrist. Sitting next to me was a man about fifty with a large soft drink that ran clear through the straw, more likely seltzer than 7-Up. Closely cut hair, black t-shirt tucked into black Levis, V-shaped torso, arms so perfectly defined he could have been a model for *Gray's Anatomy*: gay creative director for an ad agency. Behind me a well-dressed couple in their mid forties. I pegged the husband as a lawyer more by his posture than anything else. His designer casual wear was built for comfort, but the man sat like he was still wearing a suit.

Four people came in through the swing doors just as the lights went down and the theatre advertisement for the snack bar came on. They paraded down the aisle talking street level volume, but no one wanted to hear the soundtrack, anyway. The screen was telling the audience how to behave: no talking, use the trash receptacles, and for God's sake, no smoking. The four had an argument about splitting up and sitting in front or sitting all together in the back. The women just wanted to get their heads out of the projector beam. The guys wanted to sit all together, and from what I gathered it was because they only had one flask and it was in one of the women's purse. They trooped back up the aisle, the shadows of their heads enlarging as they walked. Jeans on the women were a little too tight. The t-shirts the guys wore — it was dark, I couldn't read what they said — were less a fashion statement, more a matter of what was in the bureau drawer that morning. Just as the soundtrack told us all to sit back, relax, and enjoy the show, the four I had mentally christened full-fledged members of the Bridge and Tunnel Society — people who come into Manhattan over the Brooklyn Bridge or through the Holland Tunnel from New Jersey — decided to sit in the four seats next to the lawyer and his wife. Sissy Spacek began her ingenuous narration, and after her fish died, that was the last I heard or saw of the film for the next ten minutes.

'Who goes in first?' the biggest guy said.

Sibilant shhhhhs floated up in the dark.

One of the girlfriends said, 'Just sit down. Could we just sit down?'

The biggest guy began to crawl over the legs of first the lawyer and then the lawyer's wife, but he stopped and said to the girl right behind him, 'I don't want to sit next to the wall.'

'Quiet, please.' Someone from down front.

I leaned forward a little, as though four inches would make a difference. It was going on directly behind me.

'Just sit down,' his girlfriend said.

'I don't want to sit by the wall.'

More shushing noises.

'Sit down. I'll crawl over you. Just sit down.' She'd lost her patience and the guy didn't like that. He said, 'I don't want to sit next to you, neither.' He was straddling the lawyer's wife's legs and all she could see was his belt buckle. She said, 'You're blocking my view.'

He said, 'Keep your pants on, lady.'

She said, 'Sit down.'

He said, 'On your face.'

She said, 'Why don't you go back to Brooklyn and leave us alone?'

I thought, Jeeez, lady, if you're going to play the stereo-type game, keep it to yourself. And then I leaned a little further away from my chairback, and placed my left foot in the aisle because there's a saying in New York: 'You never know who has the gun.'

The other three bustled into the row and manoeuvred themselves and their friend into a seat and just as the rustling subsided, just as I started to think about settling back again, the guy said in a voice as big as his frame, 'What I want to know, is where the FUCK you're from, lady.'

Then there was a real silence in our part of the theatre: no body movement, no leg crossing and seat shifting, no clearing of throats. I heard the jaws of the literary popcorn eater across the aisle stop mid chew. If I had cared to, I could have actually heard Martin Sheen quit his garbage collection job after he was fired, but by then it was apparent that the action was not on the screen. The man next to me put his large soft drink down on the floor between his feet and moved forward, too.

'I said, where the FUCK are you from, lady?'

I scanned the rows ahead of me looking for a seat toward the front, but I knew I wasn't brave enough to stand up and draw attention to myself that way. Instead I draped my purse strap over my head and around my shoulder just in case I had to get out fast.

The woman's husband, the lawyer, started to speak, low, reassuring, 'Look, it's a hot day and the heat's getting to everyone, so let's just all sit back, relax and enjoy the show.'

Didn't work.

'I just want to know where the FUCK you're from, lady.'

No shhhhhs. No quiet, please. Somehow that guy made a swear word feel physical. The man next to me and I exchanged glances and then looked away, like we didn't want to be caught acknowledging the tension.

'Look, it was an unfortunate thing to say, I'll admit, but it's a hot day.'

'I've had it with the weather report, asshole.'

'I don't think there's any need for rudeness.'

'I'm not from fucking Brooklyn, bitch, you got it?'

'Look, you have anything to say, you say it to me.'

I looked up at the screen just then, surprised to find a

Dave Dillinger shouting 'Look out behind you!' halfway through a western one Sunday afternoon and getting the villain right between the eyes with an air pistol slug.

(TOM RAWORTH)

movie on it.

'I'll do more than talk to you, mister.'

'Oh, yes?'

It's not easy to leap out of a tiny theatre seat, but somehow that guy who wasn't from Brooklyn moved vertically across the row, tackled the lawyer in his seat, and they both fell into the aisle.

They fought with their knees and elbows, their hands clasped together, each keeping the other's away. Their feet flailed in search of some hold. I pulled my legs in out of the aisle. An Adidas sneaker pushed off the metal arm of my chair, and together they rolled back past the last two rows. They crashed into the swing doors, which opened full out. The dark in the theatre broke open. We watched them roll together down the three steps to the lobby, and then the doors swung shut.

One of the girlfriends stood up behind me, looked at the lawyer's wife, and said, 'Real smart, lady.' More light when she left. The wife chewed her lip a moment before she found her feet and then the dark was broken one last time.

The camera moved outside the burning house to film the flames inside through the windows. The score came up. The creative director sitting next to me retrieved his seltzer and like all good New Yorkers, we both sat back in our seats, relaxed, and enjoyed the other show.

(THERESE EIBEN)

WIDE OVERCOATS FOR REAL

In a small Parisian *cinéma de quartier* my wife and I were watching one of those potboilers purporting to depict life in the criminal underworld, spiced with violence and sex of which, at the time, the French movie industry seemed to have the monopoly. Every one of the more prominent gangsters, if memory serves, wore an overcoat as wide as it was long, like the one I saw, once, on the boxer Freddie Mills at a demolition derby.

During the climactic scene a not so young maiden who,

come to think of it, was not a maiden at all, performed a striptease in front of a bald headed gang member, condemned and already tied up for having squealed to the cops. In accordance with the censorship regulations of the day her act was abortive, terminating when she bared her breasts in close proximity to the condemned man's nose. The next instant the punk slumped to the floor. In the balcony a minor disturbance dominated by an outraged 'Oh' alerted us to the fact that we had company. With the film over, the house lights came up and, as we headed for the exit, we met another couple in the aisle. The same bald head, the very same facial features: the punk had come to the pictures to protest his own demise.

(J H MATTHEWS)

WHITE SAND

Two months after the cinema came to our little village in the foothills of the Nimba mountains on the outskirts of Sanniquelle children still continued to hound me. Although the questions did not come as hard and fast as they once did, like shotgun pellets on a hunt, the questions still did come.

'So then, is it true that ice can fall from the skies? Can you eat it? Is it hard? Or is it like rain? Why do these people walk on it, surely it must hurt. Tell us again, will you please tell us the story of ice from the skies!'

The films that had kept us excited for weeks in advance were a twenty minute short on yodeling in the Swiss Alps, and a half hour documentary about the Austrian people engaged in one of their favourite pastimes, skiing. It was almost as thrilling as the day we rioted over the high price of water and broke the settlement manager's windows. Men, women and children were sitting huddled together, watching the strange antics of the whites as they walked on snow, somersaulted through the air, almost always landing on their skis. At every jump on the slopes a uniformly sharp intake of breath was heard from the crowd.

Sometimes when the move appeared to be particularly daring we, the women, clapped heartily whilst the men slapped each other on the back with unbridled gusto as though the skier's accomplishment was their own personal victory. When, now and again, the skiers tumbled down, legs splayed, staring red-faced into the eye of the camera and into our faces, we burst out laughing at these Europeans frolicking in the snow, while we sat in the heat of our night.

No one quite knew what to make of yodeling. Neither song nor ululation it was nonetheless hilarious, guaranteed to make us double over clutching our breasts and bellies. Later the children began to call every white they saw 'hee-hoooo' as in 'Yodeleyheehooo'.

When I went to their homes to drink black tea and gossip the women would ask, 'Well girl. This place where it is so cold. England. What is it like? There are buildings, we have seen in films and on picture postcards, which rise so high their tips disappear into the clouds. Is this so?'

'So high that when you reach the top you can see the face of God.'

And they would laugh, shocked that my tongue could wrap itself around such weighty words. May God forgive you, girl.

But why do these whites behave so like children in their country and here they cannot shape their faces into a smile?

'It is the heat that prevents them,' I would say.

'Ay girl, you can lie so. Where did you learn such a skill?'

'In the land of the whites.'

'This we can believe. Yes. In the land of the cinema is where you learned to lie for surely ice does not fall from the skies and that is white sand and no one, not even your whites, will see the face of God until they die.'

(NANCEE OKU BRIGHT)

Even moments of chance synchronicity in the living room serve only to prove that the true home of movies is in the cinema. Midway through a TV showing of *Moonraker* one of M's hired assassins fires a rocket launcher at the screen. Simultaneously the bulb in the standard lamp behind my head blows out: 'Bond is back! With enough power to knock out a 60 watt lightbulb!'

(IAN BREAKWELL)

EMERGO

The Regal cinema, in Caldergate, was between 1948 and 1952 the most important building in Carlisle. Forget the castle and the cathedral. When we moved to another part of the city I became unfaithful to the Regal. Young ladies were more impressed by the Lonsdale, or the City (now Little-woods) with its Doric columns. The City gave me an unrepeatable experience, more fully formed than 3D, a hologram that was solid: 'Emergo.'

Eccentric and flamboyant director William Castle's best known movie is *The Tingler*. If anyone died of fright during *Macabre*, Mr Castle promised $1000. But his ultimate gimmick was in *The House On Haunted Hill*. Vincent Price lowers a victim into a vat of boiling acid. Hoisting him out he points the pulley towards the audience, turns the handle, grins malevolently and then: Emergo! No, none of us were ready for this. From beside the screen a skeleton appeared and floated over our heads towards the exit. To the sound of cheers it teetered in the spotlight, shaking as it was bombarded with coins and cigarette packets. Some stood on seats and tried to grab its toes. Eventually it reached the end of its wire, was unhooked and tucked away until its next appearance. When William Castle had showed the prototype to Allied Artists it fell off its wire and landed on Chief of Studio Operations Eugene Arnstein. We saw the perfected model. When I stand in Littlewoods now I can trace its progress from Dairy Products over Home Baking and out through Fashions.

(ERIC WALLACE)

Vincent Price pulls Emergo's strings

A NUMBER ONE CLUB

I've watched Kenneth Anger's *Scorpio Rising* in art schools, the old ICA, the golden days of the Electric in Portobello Road, but nowhere more incongruously than very early one cold morning when, after a night's drinking and talking, half a dozen of us were wandering in central

A solipsistic golfer

London and came across The Breakfast Club, a magical oasis promising porridge, kedgeree and coffee, and this at six a.m.

We bluffed our way past membership restrictions and found ourselves in a warm, dim, tent-like interior, with a bar in the centre and tables set out to the right. While the others made a bee line for the kedgeree, my attention was caught by flickering and clacking to the left: there was a canvas lined corridor, in which one completely self-absorbed man was monotonously practising golf drives. At his end of this literal cul-de-sac an equally solitary and self-absorbed 16mm projector was hiccupping Anger's film, manifestly savaging the sprocket holes as it jerked along. No one was watching the film, as it hobbled painfully through the gate; and the solipsistic golfer didn't seem to care what his shots were aimed at.

The waitress asked me if I knew anything about projectors, and I fixed the film, so that the dinosaur antics of the bikers held steady, apart from the regular ripple caused by the impact of the golf ball.

(DAVID MACLAGAN)

SHERRY TRIFLE

Every time I see Hayley Mills I feel deeply, physically, nauseatingly ill. Still. Thirty years after the event. The event was the result of two circumstances. One, that Miss Mills was in *Whistle Down the Wind* at our local cinema. Two, the house was empty as I prepared to leave for the matinee. Unwilling to spurn the smile of divinity I liberated a bottle of VP Rich Ruby Sherry from the bottom of the wardrobe, before repairing to the Queens.

As I was seven at the time the VP needed to be disposed of swiftly and furtively. With some assistance from colleagues the bottle was empty by the end of Pathé News. When I regained consciousness I discovered myself lying among fag ends and empty ice cream tubs. I was unwell. A visit to the Gents was imperative. As I pulled my chin high

enough to rest on the wooden back of the seat in front —
mercifully unoccupied — I saw Hayley Mills and began to
retch. Fully, expansively, achingly.

In some ways I suppose I was lucky. I can handle sherry
again now. Hayley Mills makes me throw up. It could have
been the other way round.

(CHRIS PROCTOR)

Hayley Mills

AN EVENING WITH THE CORLEONES

I was alone in Los Angeles over the Christmas holidays. My
family was back east — we're from India and don't celebrate
Christmas anyway — and my friends had mostly left for
other places. Many suicides take place over the holidays:
the loneliness gets to people, the overwhelming realisation
they have no belonging. It was getting to me too. So
Christmas Eve I went to see a double bill of *The Godfather I
& II* at the New Beverley Cinema, expecting of course to be
the only one there. No. All of non-Christian L.A. was there,
packing themselves in to spend an evening with the
Corleone family. If you couldn't be with your own, this was
the next best thing.

The New Beverley Cinema is a revival house, one of the
worst kept in L.A. The floors are sticky with spilt Coke, the
springs in the seats are like dead slinkys, no jump, the place
smells fetid, and the screen has rents in it. But this is the
magic of movies: you can forget all this. You can forget that
everyone else is in the warm company of family and friends
eating good food while you are in the stink of the New
Beverley watching a lot of blood being spilt. And you can
really have yourself a good time. Grabbed by Brando,
Pacino and DeNiro, all of a sudden you're alive. You want to
get on your knees and thank the heavens above for giving
you this moment of respite from the ugly loneliness: the
closest thing you've had to a religious experience on
Christmas Eve.

(MONONA WALI)

THE END OF HISTORY

Walking down one of the oldest streets in Dieppe of an evening, our attention was caught by a torn poster on the dusty window of what had once been a café. It was headed '*Avis aux Travailleurs*' and we assumed it was some old municipal information sheet. Close up, it turned out to be considerably more exciting: a bulletin from the wartime Resistance warning people to avoid transportation to the forced labour programme in Germany, '*l'esclavage hitlérien*.' Part of the poster was missing; a corner was flapping loose; the print had faded. Pasted over another corner were the remains of another Resistance flyer, and beneath was what seemed to be German propaganda: details of reception and welfare centres in Germany for conscripted French workers. There were signs that renovation of the café had begun; no doubt the boards that originally covered the window, thus preserving these remarkable relics, had recently been removed.

But they surely wouldn't last long exposed to the sea air. We debated phoning the local paper straight away, but it was by now too dark for a photo and we decided the posters would be safe enough till the next day. Next morning we photographed them from every possible angle but held off on alerting the press. Friends were arriving from England. As soon as they disembarked we dragged them round to marvel at our discovery. More friends came the next day. One of them, a writer, was so entranced she faithfully copied every visible word, intending to incorporate it into her next piece of fiction.

By our sixth visit to the site we were becoming baffled as to why no one else in the street had noticed. Finally, seeing an elderly woman peering at us from a neighbouring window, we decided to share our treasure trove. 'Posters, Madame, from the Resistance!' She smiled, benignly, and enlightened us. A year ago, Chabrol had been filming *Une Affaire de Femmes* in Dieppe. Starring Isabelle Huppert, it was based on the true story of a Dieppe woman who was guillotined in the war for performing abortions. We'd seen the film, which had outraged some of France's militant Catholics as much as Scorsese's *The Last Temptation of*

Christ: someone had died of a heart attack after they'd thrown tear-gas grenades into a Paris cinema where it was showing. I remembered that when we saw it we could never work out which street was used for the Dieppe footage. We could now. *'Ce n'est pas de l'histoire, monsieur'*, chuckled the woman, *'c'est du cinéma.'*

(MALCOLM IMRIE & LIZ HERON)

THE HOUSE WITH BLACK WINDOWS

Up in the Western Isles we went to the Kirk three times a week, once on Wednesdays and twice on the Sabbath. Ours was a small in-bred splinter group of Presbyterians who had struggled along on the Scottish coast for nearly a century. The sea banged away at the end of the road. It rained constantly. The trees outside dripped and pattered on the graves of innumerable ancestors, slaughtered up glen and down dale in forgotten Celtic brawls. In the austere concrete church the sermons were interminable. The minister gripped his wooden plinth and roared like the MGM lion on a tape loop. We would go to hell if we had works of art in the house, if we laboured on the Sabbath and that included cooking and driving, if the women cut their hair, wore makeup or trousers. The Pope was the Anti-Christ. Cities were cesspits of debauchery and in those cesspits were silken palaces of sin, lures of the devil, where one could see lewd images of men and women together. If we went there, blistering, suppurating sores and boils would break out around our mouths and we would thirst, a thirst such as no man could imagine and there would be 'never a drop of water to cool our burning tongues'. And outside the sea mists rolled and the sheep dogs ran down the wet hills. The owls moved in circles and deer crashed antlers in the woods. The locals jumped off the pier in winter and a ghost with no face wandered the upper road. It was the 1950s but apart from tins and cars it could have been 1900. Looking over the sea in the pearly evening light I wished I lived in another house, somewhere in the islands

Don Giovanni, Losey's luxurious saunter through Mozart's opera, offers us an exceptionally full way of enjoying the world. While watching the film I couldn't ignore my big toe which, swollen and sore, urgently needed lancing. So time and again the closeup of a toe speared by a lancet invaded the screen before me, as if it were an integral part of the Loseyan montage.

(PETR KRAL)

The cinema was packed and we sat underneath the balcony. There was an incessant rain of litter. The odd face overhanging and grinning. Because there was no way of seeking revenge Ron picked up a Kia-Ora carton and hurled it at the adult head sitting in front. Then he stared blankly at the screen while the adult threatened to punctuate his life. Ron never said a word.

(RALPH HAWKINS)

of the blessed, where everything was different. Like in books.

My parents had doubts about the Church and maintained the observances largely in deference to my grandparents, some of whom were Elders or adherents, notoriously gruelling roles. We had books and pictures and some of the family had split decisively from the rigid grip of that cruel repression and become free-thinkers, bohemians, radicals. Damned, all damned! I couldn't wait. I longed for sin but to believe in sin you have to believe in the Devil and to believe in the Devil you have to believe in God. God was harsh and vengeful. He threw people onto pitchforks over small details.

In order to kick for the other team I had to go to the cinema. We moved to York and the opportunity presented itself. The cinema looked like a palace, enormous and white with domes and minarets and bits of barley sugar. It looked like pictures in books, Moorish, Turkish, Russian. Heathen pictures. I went to a barber and had a crew-cut. The grocer called me 'Sonny'. I was eleven. I knew by then that the world was full of repellent men who wanted to do painful, and what was worse embarrassing things to small girls. Presumably they all collected in cinemas. It was better to look like a boy. One June afternoon I cycled downhill. The doors of hell were heavy and I had to push them with both hands. The Pope had obviously decorated the foyer. There was a terrible magic there. A fish tank was full of orange liquid with three oranges floating on it. I had read enough to buy a ticket for upstairs. The connotations of stalls, a sort of pit, were not ones I could handle. I went up wide, soft stairs, a sacrilegious luxury, into a dark red velvet place that looked like the belly of Jonah's whale. It seemed to breathe in and out. There were stars above. When the great blood-red portières swung back I was so nervous my nails were bleeding. I must have closed my eyes in holy dread because I remember nothing till a vast blue light poured over me. It was the Pacific. It was *Blue Hawaii*. I had never seen such colours. Here in this dismal, snobby little town were sacred rivers, frangipani, the heaven's embroidered cloths. It was followed by *The Battle of the Alamo* and I stared into Richard Widmark's urgent,

American blue eyes, so different from our eyes, bleached pale grey and green from centuries of scanning the waters and the hills.

Shortly afterwards I was sent to boarding school and for different, equally incomprehensible reasons, the cinema was again forbidden. A wealthy industrialist, member of the School Board, took his spoilt daughter and her little friends to *West Side Story* in defiance of all rules. I was more sophisticated by this time and understood that the cinema existed to provide me with exotic sexual fetishes, in this case Bernardo's purple shirt. It was sinful. I could only respond to dark men.

In another two years we all had boyfriends. We could walk out with them on Saturdays and Sundays but we couldn't sit down — anywhere. Especially not in a cinema. Several of us decided to do both at once and went to a showing of *The Haunting of Hill House*. I arranged that all the girls were to time each kiss round the back of their partner's heads on their watches and compare results later. The winner would get a chocolate mousse. My boyfriend was docile and my friends distracted. As the film progressed I grew uneasy. The house was being menaced by a dead man, some sort of religious maniac. The doors began to ripple and swell as the terrible force tried to batter its way in. I was frightened. I heard the booming and thundering of a crazed, bullying voice, rising and falling in incoherent Biblical cadences. Threatening, muttering, berating and finally fading away. How many hundreds of times had I heard that demented preaching before? How well I knew the harm and madness it could engender. The house swallows the heroine. She knows she has come home.

(ELIZABETH J YOUNG)

USEFUL ULYSSES

When I was eighteen there was a sexually segregated showing of the film of James Joyce's *Ulysses*. The censor

The cinema in the Scilly Isles is showing John Wayne's *The Green Berets* to a mainly tourist audience. As the credits begin we are surprised to see a figure stride to the front and declaim, 'This film is fascist propaganda,' before disappearing through a side exit. It is Jorg, a German psychology student who always holidays in the Scillies. Now uncomfortable, we settle to the film when down the aisle strides Jorg again, to stand before us and yell, 'And you're all fascists for watching it!'

(MICK KIDD)

(photos: Paul Robinson,
1989)

had permitted it to be shown to either male or female audiences.

In the Auckland cinema there was an excited line of women waiting in the foyer. A man stood nearby, appraising the line for men dressed as women. Noticing I wasn't wearing shoes he told me to clear off. It was quite a New Zealand tradition, not to wear shoes. Indeed it was against the law not to wear them in factories, shops, pubs, to ride a motor bike, or to go to the picture theatre. I liked not wearing shoes in the city. It made the city more tactile. You could feel the texture of the cool grass, the hot pavement. I rushed out, determined not to miss the film, and ran up to the art school at the top of the hill where, under a cast in the sculpture department, I found a huge pair of men's shoes caked in plaster. I tucked them under my arm and sprinted back to the cinema. I put them on and slid them along the carpet and down the aisle. The smell inside the auditorium was so feminine, it was as if the darkness itself was female. Grandmothers, aunts, mothers, daughters all turned to stare at the clump of my male footsteps. I felt embarrassed, not at my masculine feet, but at being with so many women. In collusion with them. Identifying with men at that time, I had an almost male fear of the power of women.

By this time I had found a seat and I relaxed, caught up in the amusement of the women at the idiocy of the New Zealand censorship laws, the way life there was so controlled by the anti-intellectuals who ran the country.

I chanced to remember the film of *Ulysses* when travelling through Spain with my elder sister and my boyfriend. We had got as far as the olive groves around Zaragoza, whose turrets and Moorish domes rose up black against the setting sun. Franco was very much alive then in 1970, and his rigid control suffused every part of Spanish life. It was as if a medieval king, with his guards, garottes, dungeons and spies, had arrived from out of the past and taken the country by its throat, strangling it slowly, keeping it a child with a man's desires, stunted and broken.

We had stopped our car by the side of the sluggish River Ebro. A swim, it was decided, might clear my head, befuddled after drinking too much wine at a gipsy fair the night before. As we two girls changed into our bathing suits my boyfriend drove off to find food. We were soon thigh deep in the murky water, lit by the rays of the dying sun, when my sister turned towards the bank and then froze in fear. A group of seven or eight men were silently surrounding us. They stood in a semi circle, expressionless, clad in various shorts and undergarments. They were transfixed by my sister's bikini, which she had insisted on bringing to a country where the men did not even wear short-sleeved shirts. We could not get past the men to the bank. And even if we did our clothes were in the departed car.

Then out of the past came the film image of Bloom, the central character in *Ulysses*, leaning on a wall, sexually aroused by a girl on the beach. When she walked away he didn't follow. 'Ulysses!' I hissed at my uncomprehending sister. 'Walk to the bank, but keep in front of me. Don't turn back!' As she moved mechanically towards the men they started closing in on us, their hands trailing on the surface of the water. Like the girl in *Ulysses* I smile coyly at the men and then twist my body into one that is severely handicapped. I flail through the water, splish splash, up, sideways, down, in crab-like movements, grinning in a fiendishly maniacal way. For some seconds the men do not move. Then shame and pity and revulsion at themselves crosses their faces and they melt away and vanish, leaving my sister and me shivering on the muddy bank.

(ALYSON STONEMAN HUNTER)

STAR TURN

My brother and I sit giggling at the kitchen table. He's only nine and not very grown up. 'Shut up you two,' growls mother, back towards us, furiously mashing up potatoes. 'One of you get the knives and forks out.' We giggle on, wondering if we dare share our secret with her. Downstairs in the shed lies my bicycle with a flat tyre, evidence of the escapade.

Denham, where the film studios were housed, was a long way to cycle. Out through the suburbs of north west London, past the sprawl of the industrial estates, down the Western Avenue, over the humpbacked bridges of the canal. Quite daring for two working class kids. Today our quarry had been unstated between us, but we'd both known who it was we hoped to get a glimpse of. We'd conceived a clever plan and later, pushing our bikes round the village, knocking on doors asking different people for drinks of water, we'd succeeded in stumbling across a minor film star, Jimmy Hanley. Not very good looking, but here he was, in the flesh, standing at his back door as large as life, passing out the jug and tumblers. We hardly liked to tell him that we were really looking for John Mills! Much later, eating our cheese sandwiches in a field, traffic roaring yards from our ears, we'd discovered the air hissing out of the tyre. Never a moment of dullness in our rich life. I with blouse tied up at the waist, hair scuffed back, dark glasses on nose. My brother, always running to catch up with me, a good mate.

After supper I help with the washing up and retire to my curtained half of the shared bedroom to absorb myself in this week's *Picturegoer*. Only half an hour to go and I'll be free. I tidy myself, squinting in the bathroom mirror, wishing I dared to use makeup. Taking off the white cotton socks, putting on the high heeled shoes. Then changing my mind and putting on plimsolls, shoes stuffed into shoulder bag. Bouncing down the stairs, yelling goodbye. Mum shouting back automatically as she rakes out the boiler. 'Don't be late, you know you've got to be up early tomorrow for school.'

On the bus, looking round for friends, wondering if Moira will remember to meet me as she promised yesterday when I'd seen her at the Co-op. A number 52 bus coming now, jump on. Past the local shops, turn the corner at the school, down alongside the swimming pool until the bus stops at Kingsbury. Crowds beginning to gather as I saunter casually along the last stretch of the road, hoping that she's there. Couldn't bear to be seen on my own. I walk the queue hoping to spot her in front of me. Unlucky, I turn to join the end of the fast growing throng, staking my claim for a place

The thicket began to heave as Davy Crockett grappled with the marauding bear. Dropping my plastic flintlock I screamed and rushed up the aisle, out of the cinema and into the street, my mum in hot pursuit. And through that Birmingham suburb a little panic-stricken boy in a coonskin hat made from Aunty Dorothy's old fur coat ran all the way home.

(IAN WALKER)

outside the Gaumont. Standing there I fidget into my high heels, hiding the school shoes in my bag. Feeling better I unbutton the top button of my blouse, smooth my skirt, pull in my waist. It's Sunday night and we are all there waiting for the cinema to open.

Twenty minutes later, now nearly at the front, money ready in hand, Moira arrives. Breathlessly looking far more lovely than I (for a start she's got a straight nose), waving a ten bob note she brushes into the space beside me. At last we are at the ticket office, down the steps and into the auditorium. Looking without looking, we try to find a place to sit. We don't want to be too noticeable, but we don't want to be overlooked. On this choice will rest the remainder of the evening. We sit three rows down from the back until an usherette calls to us to show her our tickets. Shamefaced we move nearer the front, settling on the end of a row, knowing that everyone who comes past can see us, that everyone who sits in our row must brush past us.

People mill around, laughing and talking, gradually moving to their seats as music fills the air. Finally the lights go down. We sit transfixed. What has happened? No Buster Smith or Brian Baker. What's gone wrong? Have they decided to go to Neasden or to Wembley tonight? Did we get our reconnaissance wrong? They're usually here. Moira gets up to go to the toilet, a final desperate sweeping gaze at the backs of silhouetted heads, eerily lit faces. Shoving her way back in beside me, with a shake of the head, we settle down to watch the first short picture. Someone pushes past us, sitting in the seats next to me. I hiss loudly that they are reserved but get my hand sat on for my trouble. Giving up in disgust, we move to another part of the cinema.

Later, in the interval, we spot our prey. Sitting in a row with other boys and girls. Who is with who? How to proceed? Daringly, Moira sidles along the row of seated youths, half turning this way and that as she moves through, treading on toes, falling into laps, knocking heads with her handbag, picking up information like a mine-sweeper. Right through to the other end of the row, up the aisle and round the back. 'No good,' she hisses in my ear. 'I think we're too late tonight.' We sigh, fiddling and settling ourselves for the second half. Suddenly I glimpse a tall figure in a green pullover, moving past us, down towards the front. I leap out behind him, moving fast to catch him, following into the empty seats in the first row. There he sits, glasses perched, peering. I collapse into the seat beside him, accidentally brushing against his sleeve. He half looks at me. 'Can you keep this seat for me for a minute?' I gasp. Back up the aisle, grabbing Moira by the arm, dragging her down to the front. There we sit like lemons in a row, the screen looming over us, one each side of the imprisoned boy. 'Have you got a friend?' we both ask simultaneously as the lights go down and the MGM lion starts to roar.

Later, in the safety of my bedroom I call across the partition to my brother. 'He's called Barry. He's got lovely hands. Do you know who I mean?' I ask him. 'Naw,' he says in a haze of sleep.

(JO SPENCE)

DIZZY SPELLS

For a children's matinee, it was a thriller of unbearable tension, starring that shiny lipped lisper and unforgettable bad lot Gloria Grahame. It kept me literally on the edge of my seat hardly daring to look. When we left the cinema the afternoon sun hit me between the eyes with such stunning force that I reeled from an instant migraine which turned my legs to rubber and set my stomach heaving. Somehow I dragged myself up the hill and arrived home yellow faced, damp browed and ready to throw up. Mum took one look and made me lie on the front room sofa with the curtains drawn and a cold wet flannel over my eyes. The excitement and tension produced by going to the pictures was too much for me, and even now I'm not immune. But that particular migraine marks the beginning of my association of watching films with being ill.

By my late teens I was a committed picturegoer and a devoted jazz and sports fan. When the 1956 boxing movie *The Harder They Fall* arrived at the Barnet Odeon I was first in line. It starred Humphrey Bogart as a corrupt

Somebody asked me, 'When did you first see *L'Age d'or*?' In The Queen's Elm pub. In 1961 it wasn't an easy film to catch, so George Melly, who'd seen it, would recount the movie shot by shot. This was such a vivid way of seeing the film that when I viewed it later it seemed comparatively flat.

(PATRICK HUGHES)

journalist and ex-world champ Primo Carnera as the contender. I went to the afternoon show and, come the title fight, the giant Carnera's face gets cut to ribbons. The sequence went into slow motion, with the sound of the punches amplified and echo added. As I alternately opened and shut my eyes the familiar faintness began to overwhelm me. I dropped my head between my knees, like a beaten boxer on his corner stool, and breathed deeply. I lurched to my feet and made for the exit while the merciless blows rained down and the ghastly images flickered in the corner of my eyes. Somehow I made it outside and, like Carnera in the film, I wasn't actually floored.

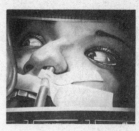

*Spanish cinema billboard
(photo: John Christie, 1988)*

Then I had a summer job working at Barnet General Hospital as a casualty ward porter and was plunged into a nightmare world of crash victims, industrial and domestic mayhem, heart attacks and distraught relatives. Ever on call, only my dread of fainting and making a dangerous fool of myself kept me conscious. I even survived a suicide from the local special hospital who'd sat on the lavatory one morning and slit his throat from ear to ear. After eight weeks I'd hardened up no end and thought myself immune to the sight of blood and gore.

However, when *Lady Sings The Blues* came out in the 1970s I took my French friend Catherine Avignon to see the biopic of Billie Holiday as her birthday treat. It was a big screen, a big sound. Finally, when Billie shoots up in the bathroom, the needle pierced her skin and I went out like a light, striking my head on the back of the seat in front of me as I pitched forward. I came to in the neon glare of the street, sitting on the pavement with my back against a brick wall. Poor birthday Kate had managed to drag me out.

(JEFF CLOVES)

MONTY

Monty was always there! Saturday night for the Derby cinemagoer in the '50s and '60s was never complete without a disruptive foray from this legendary figure. I sat in front of him during a showing of *The Servant* (Losey's great masterpiece etc. etc.) when suddenly, with encouragement from his many admirers, he stood up, screamed, and yelled 'Bollocks' into the darkness. There was the clatter of official feet but, as usual, the great man evaded capture. Leaping and diving across the half-slumbering, kissing and canoodling audience he reached the exit and made a noisy departure.

It was said that he wore disguises to gain entrance to cinemas. How else could he return after riding a bike across the stage during *Yield to the Night* at the Majestic? What chance of a welcome after removing an attendant's flat peaked cap and hurling it at a passing usherette at the Rex during the nudist classic *Isle of Levant*? Some said he was a boffin, a grammar school boy with a Jekyll and Hyde personality. Who knows? Monty, where are you now?

(KEVIN COYNE)

NANOOK STRIKES BACK

'And today we're fortunate to have the services of Steve Caplin at the piano.'

Why do people applaud before you've done anything? Makes you feel you've suddenly got something to live up to. What to do? Stand up, bow? No. Stare fixedly at the keyboard, keep your index finger on middle C? The lights will be going down soon.

The hardest part's the intro. I don't know what the first scene is, so I don't know what to play for the credits. Let me think. Snow. Igloos. Nothing springs to mind. 'White Christmas'? 'Jingle Bells'? No, maybe not. Something softer. A lilting, lyrical theme. Gentle yet hopeful. Lots of tinkly notes for the snow, but a strong bassline to herald the drama we're going to see. Whatever that might be.

The credits roll, and dissolve into the first scene. It's a snowscape. OK so far, right on target. The drama of course will come later. Let me tell you about *Nanook of the North*.

It's an hour-long film about Eskimos, early twenties. Made in black and white. Mainly white. They catch a seal. No, that's not quite all. They meet a trader. He's got a wind-up gramophone. (Ah! Good. Cue 1920s flapper music, something fast and raucous, something the Eskimos would never have heard before. The frenzied harmonies of decadent city life counterpointing the stark harshness of an Eskimo winter.)

Thirty-five minutes into the film. 'Mnng glchnm greeksk,' mouths Nanook, our hero, and the words I AM GOING TO HUNT A SEAL flash up on the screen. I am overcome by a wave of relief. At last, the plot is hotting up. A sinister bass riff builds up the drama, as more discordant harmonies add to the tension. (Nanook is cutting a hole in the snow.) The bassline gets a little faster, the harmonies a little more jarring. (Nanook drops his line in the hole.) Steady . . . a gradual strengthening of tone, some major tones creep in among the discords. (A bite! And a big one! The line tightens.) Faster goes the bass riff, brighter and stronger ring out the harmonies. (Nanook struggles with the line.) The bass is like the sound of distant drums, the harmony a half-remembered war cry. (Nanook struggles with the line.) The bass drums out a leitmotif of terrifying intensity, the harmonies break into a vibrant victory roll. (Nanook struggles with the line.) Faster and faster, the bassline becomes a Wagnerian thunderstorm matched by an explosion of harmony in tumultuous crescendo. (Nanook struggles with the line.) Faster! Louder! More! More! Ah!

All is quiet. The pianist is spent, his nerves shot, a victim to the horror of premature crescendo. Nanook struggles noiselessly with his prey. The seal makes no sound as it is dragged from the hole and beaten to death with a club of foam rubber. The pianist shivers in his own cold sweat as Nanook, triumphant, shrieks a soundless imprecation to his god.

(STEVE CAPLIN)

During John Milius's *Red Dawn* someone darted in through the exit door and threw a distress flare into the auditorium. It set fire to a seat and filled the cinema with red smoke. The manager shouted through the carmine haze, 'Turn on the lights!' but they never came on. As a tank battle developed on screen the fire brigade arrived to axe the flaming seat.

(JAMIE MUIR)

IN BARAMITA

In Baramita, Guyana, the only event of any importance, apart from the plane from the capital on Fridays, was Wesley's film show on Saturday night. Wesley Baird and I, together with anyone else who might be in town — four wooden buildings alongside a rough grass strip — would sit in the stalls, that is to say on Wesley's verandah. Drinking rum and lime and fending off the insects fighting for a place on the tiny island of the light bulb, we would chat until it was time to start. As a young man from a foreign land he was glad of my company.

Sometimes a stray remark, as for instance turning up a cheque book for the Baramita Gold Mines Inc. account, would prompt Wesley to talk of the past. He'd first come up the Baramita River thirty-five years before as a pork knocker, prospecting for gold with his father, when it took four weeks by boat and trail to get there from the coast. The gold had gone but Wesley had stayed, a big black man one half of whose face smiled slightly less than the other as the result of a stroke. Wesley would often threaten to leave Baramita, to go off up-river prospecting again, saying his life was not finished yet; but he knew that to leave his settlement meant both he and it would die.

Howler monkeys howled from the cliffs of tropical rain forest rising behind the house. From our seats we could see the single line of burning brands at the far end of the airstrip. Slowly the audience began emerging from their homes in the surrounding jungle. In daylight Wesley could recognise each one by their walk from a quarter of a mile away. Until a few years ago these Amerindians had all worked his mine. Now the only bit of equipment still functioning was Wesley's battered prewar projector. His mining gear lay in ruins, rusting in the bush like so many dreams of El Dorado. While his mine was in production it was said he'd financed more than one general election campaign and flown plane loads of friends and champagne up from the capital. 'Bullion Baird is what they used to call me,' he said, and laughed.

By now forty or fifty of his audience were waiting, drinking rice wine and chatting around the beaten earth of

Dear Son,
We have decided not
to buy a video
recorder as your
father thinks the
wiring will upset the
look of the television
table.
                    (MRS FINCH)

Wesley's yard below us. Wesley threw the switch and the projector began to grind away in his bedroom, throwing its black and white images, flecked and scratched with age, across the yard to the screen between us and the airstrip. I often wondered what the Caribs made of what they were seeing, a strange grey world none of them had ever visited, accompanied by a distorted soundtrack in a language none of them understood. They were as fascinated by the world on the screen as I was with theirs, to the surprise of the pork knockers and others I met in the bush. Films of frontier life in westerns were popular with Wesley as well as with his audience. The same film would be shown several weeks in succession, and the fight scenes three times: once, again in reverse, and once again, to applause and shouts of encouragement throughout. Most successful of all, though, was *Tarzan and his Mate*. From their rousing applause and their even louder parodying of his call Tarzan was clearly someone with whom the Amerindians could identify. Johnny Weissmuller swung on guarana ropes between silk cotton trees exactly like the ones behind the screen. He wore as few clothes as they did.

Crazed horse in foyer

Changing a reel, Wesley would complain that it was hardly worthwhile bringing the films up from Georgetown. It was difficult to get the audience to pay the few cents he demanded for the privilege. He said, 'All they do is sit on their backsides and watch the film. *I* have all the trouble and expense of ordering the films, getting them sent from the distributor to the airport by car, the freight on the plane, returning them, as well as the hire of the film. Then you are forgetting the most expensive item: myself, the projectionist and theatre manager!' We laughed, knowing that Wesley enjoyed the films more than anyone, perhaps because the showing of them was all that remained to remind him of the mining empire he once ran.

After the film was the dance. Wesley was generous, offering me a young Amerindian girl — who no doubt would one day become one of his 'wives' — in much the same way he would a rum. It gave him pleasure to have others enjoy what he did, like the reggae records he played until morning. I can still recall some of the lyrics:

It was a lesbian film with a predominately lesbian audience. As two characters discussed their own sexual preferences, my man friend coughed without covering his mouth and deposited a gob of spittle in the hair of the woman in front. Now too uncomfortable to stay we slunk out to derisive cries of 'What's the matter, guy? Can't handle it?'

(DONNA RAE)

I don't know and I don't know
Why they make people bad minded so
When you try to reach the top
They all want to see you drop.

We all danced, little children, mothers suckling their babies, young men and women, grandmothers and great grandfathers, even the presiding figure of Wesley 'Bullion' Baird himself, around and around the beaten earth of the yard between his house and the screen.

(JULIAN HENRIQUES)

BREATHLESS

Once, when you and I were almost strangers, we sat withholding lust in the Renoir cinema, struggling to follow the tortuous road through *Rocinante*. We had met before, feigned casual interest, looking, nothing happening, wanting.

Desire made unfolding images irrelevant. I was held in close darkness, aching to touch your thigh, your breath louder than voices on the screen. We remained suspended, silent. Nothing happened.

You leant forward, moaning gently as if your body could no longer contain your need. Taut static hung between us. My quivering hand reached for your bare neck and firmly massaged it. My eyes watched the screen, burning to look at you, to see you clearly.

The hero had come upon a vast English country home. Nothing happened. Excruciating moments passed.

'Annihilating all that's made/To a green thought in a green shade.'

'Marvell,' we both whispered simultaneously, words releasing tension, voices urgent.

Suddenly you asked the screen: 'Shall we stay, or go to bed?' Your brazenness thrilled me. You had said what I longed to hear, longed to speak, but feared to utter.

'What?' I checked your mouth in the half light, unsure

that you could be serious, could want me, upfront as a movie star.

'Do you want to got to bed?' You faced me for the first time.

'Yes'. The clearest, surest answer burst from me and we stood up and left.

Now, you and I are lovers. Many months later we sit in the half-full Cannon, Tottenham Court Road, *À bout de souffle* enchantingly before us. It's cold outside and your coat is over our knees. The seats on either side are empty. In the warmth, I want you. I begin to undo the belt to your trousers under the coat, carefully holding the buckle so that it does not clink.

I watch Jean Seberg. Her crisp monochrome body teases. I feel the presence of people around me and yet do not notice them. Your thighs tense. I can tell that you are aroused. Your hand is pressing between my legs, melting the wet into my jeans. I shift in my seat and tremble. I push my fingers into your knickers, the tips dance on your growing clit. You make the stifled noises of someone gagged. You move your head as if to release the sounds your lips ache to

Jean Seberg breathlessly flees a cinema

break. I test the soft wide hollow of your cunt. It drips into my hand. I can see the firm set line of your jaw, your cheeks, bitten.

I watch Jean Seberg. She is running. You are rigid. She is being chased through the streets. You are leaning back in your seat, eyes closed. She is running down the stairs of a cinema, to hide, to escape, the music growing more frantic, my fingers rubbing you, circling, stroking until you explode, silently in the dark, unkissed.

(CHERRY SMYTH)

IN THE COMPANY OF WOLVES

Once upon a time, on an island called Manhattan, I went to see a film called *The Company of Wolves* and found myself in the company of a pack of real wolves.

When the British film *The Company of Wolves* (screenplay by Angela Carter) was released a few years ago in New York City I was excited. I'm a big fan of Ms Carter's writing. And I'd read that it was a lyrical, erotic, feminist retelling of the fairy tale 'Little Red Riding Hood'. In other words, my kind of movie.

The Company of Wolves was playing in a movie house in Times Square. The kind that specializes in slash-and-gash horror films, and that caters to teenaged boys who go to the movies primarily to see virginal-looking, buxom, teenaged girls on the screen being brutally raped, killed and dismembered.

The reason that *The Company of Wolves* wasn't being shown in a tiny art cinema in SoHo or TriBecA, where it would have gotten a devoted downtown audience dressed in black and carrying semiotics textbooks under their arms, was because it was being distributed in the States as a formulaic horror film. The distributor must have seen the word 'wolves' in the title and leaped to the conclusion that it was a movie about horny young men turning into bloodthirsty werewolves, perhaps accompanied by hungry and fierce packs of real wolves, all roaming around town

I worked in a Soho building which also housed a porn cinema. The manager told me of the things they found under the seats after the shows, ranging from sticky handkerchiefs to old punters who had collapsed with heart attacks and the bruised and bloodied corpse of a rabbit which had obviously been fucked to death. But, as he said, it was a very attractive rabbit, probably 'asking for it'.

(DEBORAH ORR)

*Cinema in Times Square,
New York*

together, looking for some fresh virgin meat to sink their teeth into.

Times Square, with its theatre marquees advertising live sex shows with 'Oreo Cookie Specials', and movies with titles like *Slits and Sluts*, and its astronomically soaring crime rate, is a dangerous place, especially for women. It's not my favourite part of town.

Nevertheless, I went to the movie theatre in Times Square that Saturday night because I was determined to see what Angela Carter would do, via the medium of film, with our oh-so-precious fairy tale icon Little Red Riding Hood. When I arrived there were packs of teenaged boys standing outside the theatre. They'd come not only from Manhattan, but from all the boroughs: Brooklyn, Queens, Staten Island and the Bronx. It was a melting pot: tough-looking white boys in black leather jackets; tough-looking Hispanic boys in army fatigues; and tough-looking black boys in skin-tight, silver colored lycra shorts. And they were all excited. In many cases, their excitement was drug induced, I was pretty sure of that. 'Wolves!' they kept shouting to one another. 'Man, I like wolf movies!' 'Eat them bitches up,' I heard one of the boys say to his friend, who nodded in

A gristly footnote to the scene in *Raging Bull* where Jake La Motta's face is pounded into pulp by Sugar Ray Robinson was revealed when I went to the Gents and discovered I'd been sitting on a meat pie left on the seat and which was stuck to the seat of my pants.

(IAN BREAKWELL)

ferocious agreement. 'Dig their teeth,' another said.

I tiptoed into the theatre, head down, trying not to look any more conspicuous than I already did as a solitary adult female wearing a black jersey dress, dangling silver earrings, and bright red lipstick. I sat way in the back.

After about fifteen minutes of coming attractions (all advertising movies in which blonde sorority girls are savagely murdered by hulking, psychotic-looking men) *The Company of Wolves* began. During the credits, the audience was so noisy, so excited, that I could hardly see the screen or hear what was going on. The boys were standing, throwing junk food at each other, yelling, threatening to turn the wolves on one another. They were ready for a good time.

Finally, about half of the boys in the audience sat down, and I craned my neck every which way, hoping to catch what was happening on the screen. At the beginning of the movie, if I can remember (and I may not be remembering it at all the way it is), there's a young innocent female child traipsing through the woods, and then, someone is transformed, slowly and evocatively, into a wolf. The boys in the audience were howling. Man, they knew what to expect, they knew the formula inside out. If someone turns into a wolf, the wolf is going to brutally dismember, and then devour, a young girl. And there will be blood. Lots and lots of bright red virgin blood. Still, virgin blood or not, the boys knew one other thing, too: if the girl was walking somewhere by herself where the wolf was free to get at her, then clearly she was asking for it and had gotten no more than she deserved. 'Kill her ass!' the boys were shouting out to the screen. 'Screw her buns off!' 'Eat her titties!' 'Destroy the mother!' By then, at least, nearly all of them had sat down, eager for the blood to start pouring on the screen.

But there was no dismemberment. No blood. What there was instead was a lyrical, dreamy sequence. The boys were growing confused. Their excited shouts turned into annoyed grumbling. This movie wasn't following the formula they knew and loved so well, the formula they had every reason to expect. After all, nobody had told them that this was really a postmodern, lyrical, feminist film that should have been showing at the Film Forum or the

Bleecker Street Cinema (theatres they'd undoubtedly never heard of). And even if someone had told them, they still wouldn't have understood, or cared. 'Postmodern' and 'lyrical' were not words that would have had much meaning to them. 'Feminist' might have, although it probably would have evoked the image of some short-haired 'dyke' who they would have been more than thrilled to brutally dismember, themselves, *gratis*, you name the time and place, they'll be there.

Twin usherettes

In any case, could I really blame them for not knowing what to expect from a film by Angela Carter? They knew exactly what gave them pleasure in cinemagoing, just as I knew exactly what gave me pleasure. And many of them had traveled a long distance on the filthy, dangerous subway to get to the theatre — a lot worse a ride than my ten minute hop by bus — and they'd paid real money to obtain that pleasure. Why should they be denied?

Still, since it was just the beginning of the movie, the boys were willing to wait a little longer for the blood and gore, if they had to. Maybe this movie was just slow to start. Besides, soon enough someone else onscreen was turning into a wolf. Or maybe it was the same person. I was having a difficult time following anything other than what was going on in the audience. Because this time when their expectations were not met, and another dreamy forest sequence was shown instead of a dismemberment, they were slower to settle down. 'This is fucking bullshit,' I heard one of them say. 'What kind of fucked-up movie is this?' asked another. I, of course, knew the answer. But I held my tongue.

Well, after a few more lush, lyrical sequences the boys had had enough. They were good sports, sure, but life was just too short for them to have to endure an evening like this. They stood up. They began shouting and stomping their feet. There were shouts, curses, and threats. 'Fuck this motherfucking bullshit jive-ass movie!' was a line I kept hearing. 'These fucking assholes better give me back my fucking money!' and 'This ain't no wolf movie!' were two others. My favourite, though, was 'Your momma eats wolves' titties!'

Unless the boys got back their motherfucking money it

I'm walking gingerly backwards down the aisle, selling ice creams from a tray. We're showing Buster Keaton in a film where the side of a house falls on him. Just as the wall topples my heel catches and I keel over. I hit the deck the instant the wall slams into the ground. Cornets land on my chest and slide down my nylon overall. Keaton survives unharmed.
(SYLVIA HARKINSON)

was clear, at least to me, exactly what was going to occur: a bona fide riot. Naturally, I wasn't eager to find myself in the midst of a riot for no good cause. Especially since, as the only member of the audience wearing lipstick, I felt particularly vulnerable. Besides, all I wanted was to see the movie. And I was, by that time, feeling a real sense of urgency about seeing it, since it was also becoming clear to me that *The Company of Wolves* was going to close very quickly. This might be my last chance to see it. So, despite the shouts and threats of the boys running in packs through the aisles and stomping their feet and cursing and pushing and shoving one another, I remained determinedly in my seat, still craning my neck every which way, still valiantly trying to see the screen.

After a few more minutes, though, I couldn't stand the suspense of not knowing what was going on in the lobby of the theatre. I tiptoed out to the lobby, where I saw the terrified-looking ticket takers wildly handing out five-and ten-dollar bills, whatever denomination they could lay their hands on, in order to appease and quiet the boys. Feeling slightly reassured that a real riot wasn't going to erupt, I tiptoed back to my seat. And, throughout all of this, none of the boys in the audience ever spoke to me, or even seemed to look at me. My presence in the theatre must have been so impossible for them to imagine that I was rendered invisible. And I actually managed to sit calmly through the rest of the movie, although I was never able to concentrate on it.

When I look back at that Saturday night I understand that I had witnessed something magnificent: a fairy tale gone completely awry, an audience that had transformed itself into its very own horror movie, its very own company of wolves.

(JANICE EIDUS)

Some way through the film a man got up to go to the Gents, which was next to the screen. He walked along in front of it just as a train was roaring along in the opposite direction, so appearing to be battling against the oncoming locomotive to get to the lavatory. When he finally reemerged the audience applauded him. He had no idea why.

(ANDY COLE)

AMERICAN PRESENCE IN SOUTH KEN

I don't mind when, called to the door by a knock, I discover there are a couple of missionaries outside; I even feel flattered, a misplaced emotion no doubt, that these foot-sore people would wish to convert me to their holy throng. My friend isn't so lenient. There was an occasion when we were interrupted by a couple of Jehovah's Witnesses. John went to the door while I remained in the kitchen. I didn't want any part of the scene, which was bound to be undignified. He was gone several minutes before he returned, red-faced and biting his pipe in a ferocious grimace.

'One of them was lurking round the corner, didn't come to the door with the woman who did all the talking. I saw them earlier through the window; a tall woman with a crippled bloke on crutches. I didn't like the look of him at all, looked like an ex-detective. He's left that gang and joined another. God! I could kick him in the balls for a long time without getting bored.'

John's a bit excessive. So to get the full benefit of a chat with these evangelical types I have to go out and find them. It's no good at home; John is bound to come along and spoil it. I enjoy my experiences with the missionaries because it is like a chaste courtship. I play hard to get while the suitors are alternately tender and pressing. It is so satis-

On screen a crazed killer terrorises a cinema auditorium while simultaneously in front of the screen another madman fires indiscriminately into the audience watching the movie. Bigas Luna's Anguish, 1987

fying to be the focus of such concern. It is even better with your eyes closed. What I mean is that it is quite rare to find a missionary with an attractive physique. They often look unhealthy, grey from tramping the streets and suppressing their urges. The glorious exceptions to that rule are the Mormons! Their missionaries are nearly always good-looking young American boys, aged about nineteen to twenty-three and with that trembling innocence. But this courtship, you have already guessed, is not one way; it is the job of the one being wooed to lead the suitor while making him believe that it is he who is in control. Sometimes I've abruptly revealed that it is I who have called on him which provokes a moment of delicious embarrassment: 'We-ell, I don't know. I'm just a farm boy from Saint George, Utah'.

The Mormons love a spectacle, they love to impress. They share that with the Soviets: both indulge in grandiose displays of folksiness. How well they combine the heroic with the homespun is a matter of opinion, but the effort is admirable and touching. Once or twice I have bathed in a whole day of Mormonism.

In Exhibition Road, South Kensington, there is the Jesus Christ Church of Latter Day Saints Visitors' Center. One beautiful day in July I left the sunshine and entered that windowless bunker. I saw windows before I went in, but was unaware of them once inside. First of all I was greeted by a smart sixtyish matron who suggested that I might like to see a film called *The Search for Happiness*. It began with a view through a Vaseline smeared lens of a world of nodding flowers through which smiling, healthy families of three generations passed without breaking a blade of grass. Then a splendid specimen of American manhood appeared, brooding, his expansive brow furrowed in an unconvincing display of perplexity, and as he rested his brick like chin in his cupped hands, his elbows resting on the rustic fencing of a bridge, he contemplated his image in the water below. 'Where do you come from? Where are you going?' intoned the gravelly voiceover. Unspoken, un-voiced, he knew where he was, who he was and what he was. This was why his perplexity was so unconvincing, he was confident in himself, he didn't give a damn about his

I have climbed out of Ward's Irish Pub in Piccadilly and gone into the next door cinema to sleep off the booze and woken up in the middle of a riot and after flailing my arms about realised the riot was in the film and I have sat down and gone to sleep again among the sad and indifferent junkies.

(ARTHUR MOYSE)

past or his future. But this physical exuberance didn't last long; it dissolved into lilac and turquoise mists. Effects like that are rather crude, lack subtlety. The previous scene had so many undercurrents and possible interpretations that the astral mists and disembodied spirits seemed gross. But perhaps that part should be experienced like washing your hands with a strongly perfumed soap after masturbation. The next scene was chillingly clinical. The spirit people were born into this world via a laboratory that would not have looked out of place at NASA. The filmmaker's idea of continuity was disconcerting. How were we supposed to reconcile the waving fields of flowers with this mechanised birth? By now my attention was beginning to wander. The disadvantage of a film is that it is talking to anybody. By talking to a Mormon I can, at least, change the subject when the conversation becomes ridiculous. From here onwards I was an uncomfortable witness to a procession of images celebrating American middle class complacency and bad taste. I visited horrible colonial-style interiors cluttered with enormous frilly lampshades under which sat gramps, *Book of Mormon* on one knee and little granddaughter on the other. But time was running out for gramps. We saw him die and reunite with grandma in the lilac and turquoise mists. As far as I was concerned the film had gone off the boil after the baseball playing Narcissus.

And I was not to recover that early delight. In the carpeted foyer, which was long and wide and hung with framed images of baptisms, a voyage over stormy seas, a catastrophic earthquake orchestrated by a levitating Jesus above an Aztec city, and team photos of the Mormon patriarchs, I was joined by the sixtyish matron. The boredom we both shared was tangible for a moment as she silently considered what to do with me next. There was a question on her face as to whether I really did want anything else. She sensed that I was not a potential convert.

A balding office worker came out of the little curtained-off area, and my guide remembered: 'Would you like to see the diorama?' Behind the curtain, where there was even less light than in the foyer, stood a shadowy edifice resembling a fairground booth. It resolved itself into two miniature house shaped halves between which rose a stubby artificial

Go in with a jamjar and come out with a brown jumper [a flea].
(NORTHERN SAYING)

137

tree. A faint glow filled the window at the front of each house. Another rectangle, unilluminated, hung in the tree. The guide pressed a switch and left me. There was a ticking sound, like that of a chain passing over a toothed wheel, and the rectangle in the tree folded out towards me to reveal a doll, like a ventriloquist's dummy, sitting in the branches. Its face was a low definition TV image of a boy's face framed in the metal hair and ears of the doll. The whirring stopped and was superseded by a recorded voice. 'Hi there!' it began and the flickering of the face synchronised with the monologue, which continued with the fluent casualness of the beach photographer and con man. This mechanical icon embodied completely and grotesquely the American notion of cuteness. It was truly Frankenstein Junior, weaned on Coca Cola, delivering his homilies about the joys of 'Family Home Evenings' and saving his neighbours from 'not helping one another'. The screens on the front of the little houses now showed stills of the two families. The neighbours finally joined the Osmonds for a 'Family Home Evening'. 'I don't think they wanted to, but my father's a pretty persuasive talker.'

'God bless America!' said someone behind me. It was a tall, young man in an American university sweatshirt. We stepped out into the relative light of the foyer. My hitherto unseen companion had an ironic smile. 'Embarrassing, huh?' Before I could agree we were approached by an elderly man in a grey suit which matched his dim grey eyes. During his speech the young man departed, but sometime next week I'll get a visit from a couple of young missionaries. I hope John will be out.

(DAVID CUTHBERT)

The Mean Machine at the Clapham Ruby. The chant of the prisoners - 'mean machine, mean machine' - is taken up by the audience. As the climactic game of American football gets underway the whole stalls are standing, cheering, shaking fists. During the lull of half time a traditionalist amongst us leads us into 'Abide With Me'.
(CHRIS PROCTOR)

THE PICTURES

He wasnt really watching the picture he was just sitting there wondering on things; the world seemed so pathetic the way out was a straight destruction of it, but that was fucking daft, thinking like that; a better way out was the destruction of himself, the destruction of himself meant the destruction of the world anyway because with him not there his world wouldnt be either. That was better. He actually smiled at the thought; then glanced sideways to see if it had been noticed. But it didnt seem to have been. There was a female sitting along the row who was greeting. that was funny. He felt like asking her if there was a reason for it. A lot of females gret without reason. The maw was one. So was the sister, she gret all the time. She was the worst. Whenever you caught her unawares that was what would be happening, she would be roaring her eyes out. The idea of somebody roaring their eyes out, their eyes popping out their sockets because of the rush of water. Or maybe the water making them slippery inside the sockets so they slipped out, maybe that was what it was, if it was anything even remotely literal. No doubt it would just prove to be a total figure of speech: eyes did not go popping out of sockets. There was a sex scene playing, the female one raising the blanket to go down as if maybe for oral intercourse, as if maybe she was going to suck him. Maybe this is why the woman was greeting along the row; maybe she once had this bad experience where she was forced into doing that very selfsame thing, years ago, when she was at a tender age, or else just it was totally against her wishes maybe. And she wouldnt want reminding of it. And look what happens, in she comes to see a picture in good faith and innocence, and straight away has to meet up with that terrible ancient horror

or else she enjoyed her feelings of anguish and had come along because of it, a kind of masochism or something, having heard from one of her pals about the sort of explicit — and maybe even exploitative — sex scenes to expect if she did. That was the director to blame anyway. In the pictures he was involved in something like this usually happened, and there was usually violence as well, like in this one murder. And people would end up in bad emotional states. Was it right that it should be like this? It was okay for somebody like him — the director — but what about other folk, ordinary folk, them without the security, the overall security, the ones that actually went to watch his fucking pictures! The thought was enough to make you angry but it was best to just find it funny if you could, if you could manage it. He nodded and started grinning — it was best to. But it wasnt funny at all in fact it was quite annoying, really fucking annoying, and you could get angry about it, the way these bastards in the film industry got away with it.

And there was that female now, her along the row. He felt like shouting to her: What's up missis? Something wrong?

God Almighty but, the poor woman, maybe there was something bad up with her; he felt like finding out, maybe he should ask, maybe it was some bastard in a chair nearby, maybe wanking or something because of the sex scene, and here was the woman within perception distance — listening distance — having to put up with it, and it maybe reminding her of a terrible time when she was younger, just a lassie, and was maybe forced into some sort of situation, some kind of similar kind of thing. So fucking awful the way lassies sometimes get treated.

But it had to come back to the director, he it was to blame, it was this movie making the guy wank in the first place, if he hadnt been showing the provocative sexy scenes it wouldnt be fucking happening. There was a lot to be said for censorship. If a censor had seen this he would have censored it and then the woman maybe wouldnt be greeting. But no, it was more serious than that. Definitely. It was. She was definitely greeting for a reason, a real reason, she had to be — it was obvious; it had just been going on too long. If it had stopped once the scene changed then it would have been different, but it didnt. And the female actor was back up the bed and her and the guy were kissing in the ordinary mouth to mouth clinch so if the oral carry on had been the problem it was all over now and the woman should have been drying her tears. So it was obviously serious and had nothing to do with sex at all — the kind that was up on the screen at least. Maybe he should ask her, try to help. There were no attendants about. That was typical of course for matinee programmes, the management aye worked short handed, cutting down on overheads and all the rest of it. This meant attendants were a rarity and the audience ran the risk of getting bothered by idiots.

Once upon a time a lassie he knew was a cinema attendant. She used to have to walk down the aisle selling ice creams, lollipops and popcorn at the interval; and they tried to get her to wear a short mini skirt and do wee curtseys at the customers. But they obviously didnt know this lassie who was a fucking warrior, a warrior. She quite liked wearing short mini skirts but only to suit herself. If she wanted to wear them she would wear them, but it was only for her own pleasure, she would please herself. She used to get annoyed with the management for other reasons as well; they used to get her to wear this wee badge with her name on it so it meant all the guys looked at it and knew what it was and they shouted it out when they met her on the street. Heh Susan! Susaaaaan! And then they would all laugh and make jokes about her tits. It was really bad. And bad as well if you were out with her if you were a guy because it meant you wound up having to get involved and that could mean a doing if you were just one against a few. She was good too, until she fucked off without telling him. He phoned her up one night at tea-time and she wasnt in, it was her flatmate. And her flatmate told him she had went away, she had just went away. She had been talking about it for a while but it was still unexpected when it happened. Probably Manchester it was she went to. He had his chance. He could have went with her. She hadnt asked him, but he could have if he had wanted. It was his own fault he hadnt, his own fault. She had gave him plenty of opportunities. So it was his own fault. So he never heard of her again. It was funny the way you lost track of folk, folk you thought you would know for life; suddenly they just werent there and you were on your ownsome. This seemed to happen to him a lot. You met folk and got on well with them but over a period of time yous drifted away from each other — the same as the guys you knew at school, suddenly yous never even spoke to each other. That was just that, finished, fucking zero. It was funny. Sometimes it was enough to make you greet. Maybe this was what was up with the female along the row, she was just lonely, needing somebody to talk to God he knew the feeling, that was him as well — maybe he should just actually lean across and talk to her. Could he do that? So incredible an idea. But it

During a Hammer horror film a yell of terror went up from the back. 'I felt something crawling down my neck,' explained Cyril, 'and curling round my face, then everything went dark.' Due to damp, a length of crinkled peeling wallpaper had unfurled itself from the wall and slowly dropped down, enveloping poor Cyril in the seat below.

(CHRIS GARRATT)

SEEING IN THE DARK

**Every Saturday
afternoon Terry's
father came to pick
him and his brother
up from their
estranged mother's
house. Every
Saturday he would
play the part of dad
as best he could. But
having nothing to
say to them he
always took the boys
to the pictures. After
the final credits they
would wake him.
Then he'd take them
home.**

(CHRIS PROCTOR)

was known as communication, you started talking to some-body, your neighbour. Communication. You took a deep breath and the rest of it, you fucking just leaned across and went 'Hullo there!' Except when it's a male saying it to a female it becomes different. She had the hanky up at the side of her eyes. She looked fucking awful. He leaned over a bit and spoke to her:

Hullo there missis. Are you okay?

The woman glanced at him.

He smiled. He shrugged and whispered, You were greeting and eh . . . you alright?

She nodded.

I couldnt get you something maybe, a coffee or a tea or something, they've got them at the foyer . . .

She stared at him and he got a sudden terrible dread she was going to start screaming it was fucking excruciating it was excruciating you felt like stuffing your fingers into your ears, he took a deep breath.

There wasnt anybody roundabout except an old dear at the far end of the row. That was lucky.

Maybe there *was* something up with her right enough. Or else maybe she was fucking mental — mentally dis-turbed — and just didnt have anywhere to go. Genuine. Poor woman. God. But folk were getting chucked out on the street these days; healthy or unhealthy, it didnt matter, the powers-that-be just turfed you out and they didnt care where you landed, the streets were full of cunts needing looked after, folk that should have been in nursing homes getting cared for. She was maybe one of them, just in here out of the cold for a couple of hours peace and quiet. And then look at what she has to contend with on the bloody screen . . .! God sake! In for a couple of hours peace and quiet and you wind up confronting all sorts of terrible stuff in pictures like this one the now. Maybe censors were the answer. Maybe they would safeguard folk like this woman. But how? How would they do it, the censors, how would they manage it? No by sticking the cinemas full of Walt Disney fucking fairyland. Who would go for a start? No him anyway, he hated that kind of shite. Imagine paying the entrance fee for that, fucking cartoons. He leant across:

You sure you dont want a coffee?

She shut her eyes, shaking her head for a moment. She wasnt as old as he had thought either. She laid the hand holding the hanky on her lap and the other hand she kept at the side of her chin, her head now tilted at an angle. She kept looking at the screen.

I was going to get one for myself. So I could get one for you while I was at it?

She turned to face him then; and she said, Could you?

Aye, that's what I'm saying.

Thanks, you're a pal.

Milk and sugar?

Just milk.

He hesitated but managed to just get up, giving her a swift smile and not saying anything more, just edging his way along the row. He had to pass by the old dear sitting in the end seat and she gave him a look before holding her shopping bags in to her feet to let him past, and he nodded to her quite briskly. He walked up the aisle and down the steps, pushing his way out into the corridor. Thick carpets and dim lighting. He grinned suddenly, then began chuckling. How come he had nodded at her like that? She was as old as his grannie! God Almighty! But it was to show her he was relaxed. That was how he had done it, that was how he had done it. If he hadnt been relaxed he would never have bloody managed it because it would have been beyond him.

Cinema 2 was showing a comedy. He had seen it a week ago. He wasnt that keen on comedies, they were usually boring. He continued past the corridor entrance. There was an empty ice cream carton sitting on the floor in such a way you felt somebody had placed it there intentionally. Probably they had. He used to have the selfsame habit when he was a boy — thirteen or something — he used to do things to make them seem like accidental events. If he was smoking and finished with the fag he would stick it upright on the floor to make it look like somebody had just tossed it away and it had landed like that as a fluke.

He used to go about doing all sorts of stupid things. Yet when you looked at them, they werent all that fucking stupid.

What else did he used to do? He used to leave stuff like empty bottles standing on the tops of stones and boulders,

'Cinema', drawing by Maggi Hambling, 1976

but trying to make it look like they had just landed that way accidentally. To make folk imagine alien things were happening here on planet Earth and they were happening for a reason, a purpose.

He was a funny wee cunt when he was a boy. Looking back you had to admit it.

The woman at the kiosk passed him the change from the till; she was in the middle of chatting with the cashier and didnt watch him after she had put the money on the counter so he lifted a bar of chocolate, slid it up his jacket sleeve. One was plenty. He took the two wee containers of milk and the packet of lump sugar for himself.

It was raining outside. He could see folk walking past with the brollies up. And the streetlights were on. It would soon be teatime.

He didnt take the chocolate bar from his sleeve until along the corridor and beyond Cinemas 1 & 2, which were the most popular and had the biggest auditoriums — but there were usually cunts talking in them, that was the drawback, when you were trying to listen to the movie, they held conversations, fucking conversations. He had to lay the cartons of coffee down on the floor, then he stuck his hand in his side jacket pocket, letting the bar slide straight in from the sleeve. He was going to give it to the woman. He wasnt that bothered about chocolate himself. And anyway, in his experience females liked chocolate more than males. They had a sweet tooth.

That was one of these totally incredible expressions, a sweet tooth. What did it actually mean? He used to think it meant something like a soft tooth, that you had a tooth that was literally soft, made of something like soft putty. When he was a boy he had a sweet tooth. But probably all boys had sweet tooths. And all lassies as well. All weans the world over in fact, they all liked sweeties and chocolate, ice cream and lollipops, popcorn.

She was sitting in a semi motionless way when he got back to the seat and it was like she was asleep, her eyelids not flickering at all. Here's your coffee, he said, milk with no sugar, is that right?

Ta.

He sat down in his old seat after an eternity of decision

Belfast. We come in from The Avenue, escape at the movies and unwind in the dark. Rod Steiger, munitions expert, is out to get even. The story is Irish. We've come to see Belfast, the streets, ourselves. Will he survive? You could heard a pin drop. Will the *cinema*? The shell of a building plays fiction and fact. He self-destructs. We bear the mark.

(ALASTAIR MACLENNAN)

making to do with whether or not he could just sit down next to her, on the seat next to hers; but he couldnt, it would have been a bit out of order, as if just because he had bought her a fucking coffee it gave him the right of trying to sit next to her and chat her up, as if he was trying to get off with her — which is what women were aye having to put up with. The best people to be women were men because of the way they were, the differences between them, their sexuality, because they could get sex any time they like just about whereas men were usually wanting it all the time but couldnt fucking get it — it was a joke, the way it worked like that, a joke of nature, them that wanted it no getting it and them that didnt want it having to get it all the time. The bar of chocolate. He took it out his pocket and glanced at it; an aero peppermint; he passed it across, having to tap her elbow because she was staring up at the screen.

Here. It's a spare one. He shrugged, I'm no needing it. I'm no really a chocolate lover anyway, to be honest, I've no got a sweet tooth. He shrugged again as he held it to her.

Oh I dont want that, she said out loud, her nose wrinkling as she frowned, holding up her hand to stop him. And he glanced sideways to see if folk had heard her and were maybe watching. He whispered:

How no? It's alright.

Oh naw pal I just don't eat them — aero peppermints — any kind of bar of chocolate in fact, being honest, I dont eat them.

Is it a diet like?

Aye. Thanks for the coffee but.

That's alright.

You're no offended?

Naw. I'll eat it myself. On second thoughts I'll no. I'll keep it for later. He stuck it back into his pocket and studied the screen while sipping the coffee which was far too milky it was like water. Funny, how they said something was coffee and then sold you a cup of fucking water with just a splash — a toty wee splash — of brownstuff, to kid you on. Total con. They did the selfsame thing with tea, they charged you for tea with milk and water and another wee splash of brown, a different tasting one. You couldnt trust them. But

Cinema Garage, Wakefield
(photo: Bill Coates)

it was hard to trust people anyway, even at the best of times. You were actually daft if you trusted them at all. At any time. How could you? You couldnt. Cause they aye turned round and fucked you in some way or another. That was his experience.

The film would soon be done, thank God. It was a murder picture, it was about a guy that was a mass murderer, he kills all sorts of folk. A good looking fellow too, handsome, then he goes bad and starts all the killing, women mainly, except for a couple of guys that get in his way, security men in the hostel, it was a nurses' hostel, full of women, and a lot of them fancy him, the guy, the murderer, he gets off with them first, screws them, then after he's screwed them he kills them — terrible. And no pity at all.

But sometimes you could feel like murdering somebody yourself in a way, because people were so fucking awful at times, you helped them out and nothing happened, they just turned round and didnt thank you, just took it like it was their due. His landlord was like that, the guy that owned the house he stayed in, he was a foreigner, sometimes you helped him out and he didnt even thank you, just looked at you like you were a piece of shite, like you were supposed to do it because you stayed in one of his fucking bedsits, as if it was part of your fucking rent or something.

He was sick of the coffee, he leaned to place the carton

on the floor beneath the seat. He grimaced at the woman. She didnt notice, being engrossed in the picture. To look at her now you wouldnt credit she had been greeting her eyes out quarter an hour ago. Incredible, the way females greet, they turn it off and turn it on. He was going straight home, straight fucking home, to make the tea, that was what he was going to fucking do, right fucking now. Hamburger and potatoes and beans or something, chips. He was starving. He had been sitting here for two hours and it was fucking hopeless, you werent able to concentrate. You came to the pictures nowadays and you couldnt even get concentrating on the thing because

because it wasnt worth watching, that was the basic fact, because something in it usually went wrong, it turned out wrong, and so you wound up you just sat thinking about your life for fuck sake and then you started feeling like pressing the destruct button everything was so bad. No wonder she had been fucking greeting. It was probably just cause she was feeling so fucking awful depressed. About nothing in particular. You didnt have to feel depressed about something, no in particular, because there was so much of it.

The bar of chocolate in his pocket. Maybe he should just eat it himself for God sake! He shook his head, grinning, sometimes he was a fucking numbskull. Imagine but, when he was a boy, leaving all these dowps lying vertical like that, just so somebody passing would think they had landed that way! It was funny being a wean, you did these stupid things. And you never for one minute thought life would turn out the way it did. You never for example thought you would be sitting in the pictures waiting for the afternoon matinee to finish so you could go fucking home to make your tea, to a bedsitter as well. You would've thought for one thing that you'd have had a lassie to do it for you, a wife maybe, cause that's the way things are supposed to be. That was the way life was supposed to behave. When you were a boy anyway. You knew better once you got older. But what about lassies? Lassies were just so totally different. You just never fucking knew with them. You never knew what they thought, what they ever expected. They always expected things to happen and you

Children watching Way to the West, *Hull, 1950s*

never knew what it was, these things they expected, you were supposed to do.

What age was she? Older than him anyway, maybe thirty, thirty-five. Maybe even younger but it was hard to tell. She would've had a hard life. Definitely. Okay but everybody has a hard life. And she was on a diet. Most females are on a diet. She wasnt wearing a hat. Most females were these days, they were wearing hats, they seemed to be, even young lassies, they seemed to be as well; it was the fashion.

The more he thought about it the more he started thinking she might be on the game, a prostitute. He glanced at her out the side of his eye. It was definitely possible. She was good looking and she was a bit hard, a bit tough, she was probably wearing a lot of make-up. Mostly all females wore make-up so you couldnt really count that. What else? Did she have on a ring? Aye, and quite a few, different ones, on her different fingers. She shall have music wherever she goes. Rings on her fingers and rings on her toes. Bells on her toes. She had black hair, or maybe it was just dark, it was hard to see properly because of the light; and her eyebrows went in a high curve. Maybe she *was* on the game and she had got a hard time from a punter, or else somebody was pimping for her and had gave her a doing, or else telt her he was going to give her one later, if she didnt do the business, if she didnt go out and make a few quid. Maybe her face was bruised. Maybe she had got a right kicking. And she wouldnt have been able to fight back, because she was a woman and wasnt strong enough, she wasnt powerful enough, she would just have to take it, to do it, what she was telt, to just do it. God Almighty. It was like a form of living hell. Men should go on the game to find out what like it was, a form of living hell — that's what it was like. He should know, when he was a boy he had once went with a man for money and it was a horror, a horror story. Except it was real. He had just needed the dough and he knew about how to do it down the amusements, and he had went and fucking done it and that was that. But it was so bad, a horror, a living hell. Getting gripped by the wrist so hard you couldnt have got away, but making it look like it was natural, like he was your da maybe, marching you into the toilet, the public toilet. Getting marched into the

public toilet. People seeing you as well, other guys, them seeing you and you feeling like they knew, it was obvious, him marching you like that, the way he was marching you. Then the cubicle door shut and he was trapped, you were trapped, that was that, you were trapped, and it was so bad it was like a horror story except it was real, a living hell, because he could have done anything and you couldnt have stopped him because he was a man and he was strong and you were just a boy, nothing, to him you were just nothing. And you couldnt shout or fucking do anything about it really either because

because you were no just fucking feart you were in it along with him, you were, you were in cahoots, you were in cahoots with the guy, that was what it was, the bad fucking bit, you were in cahoots with him, it was like you had made a bargain, so that was that. But him gripping you the way he was! What a grip! So you had to just submit, what else could you do, you had to just submit, you couldnt scream nor fuck all. Nothing like that. Men coming into the urinals for a pish, no knowing what was going on behind the door and him breathing on you and feeling you up, and grabbing you hard, no even soft, no even caring if he had tore your clothes. What the wonder was that nobody could hear either because of the rustling noises the way he had you pressed against the wall and then you having to do it to him, to wank him, him forcing your hand and it was like suffocating him forcing his chest against your face and then coming over you, no even telling you or moving so you could avoid it it was just no fair at all, all over your shirt and trousers, it was terrible, a horror story, because after he went away you had to clean it all up and it wouldnt wipe off properly, all the stains, the way it had sunk in and it was like glue all glistening, having to go home on the subway with it: broad daylight.

For a pile of loose change as well. How much was it again? No even a pound, fifty stupid pence or something, ten bob. Probably no even that, probably it was something like forty pee, he just stuck it into his hand, some loose change. What did prostitutes get? what did they get? women, back then, nine year ago. It was probably about five quid if it was a short time; a tenner maybe if it was all night. That was

Films mistitled in newspapers by slipshod typographers, such as *Attila the Nun* **and Truffaut's** *L'Enfant Sausage,* **could never hope in reality to live up to my imagined scenarios.**

(Ian Breakwell)

During the intermission the man behind me in the Gents was frantically pounding the Durex machine. 'Nothing like a good old bang,' another man observed. There was a crack and I turned to see the commentator splayed against the wall, blood pouring from his nose.

(DEREK SMITH)

enough to make anybody greet. But you could spend your life greeting, like his fucking sister. Because that was the thing about it, about life, it was pathetic, you felt like pressing the destruct button all the time, you kept seeing all these people, ones like the woman, the old dear at the end of the row, plus even himself as a boy, you had to even feel sorry for him, for himself, when he was a boy, you had to even feel sorry for yourself, yourfuckingself. What a fucking joke. A comedy. Life was a comedy for nearly everybody in the world. You could actually sympathise with that guy on the screen. You could, you could sympathise with him. And he was a mass murderer.

He glanced at the woman along the row and smiled at her, but then he frowned, he glared. You shouldnt be sympathising with a mass murderer. You shouldnt. That was that fucking director's fault. That happened in his pictures, you started feeling sympathy for fucking murderers. How come it wasnt for the victims. They were the ones that needed it. No the actual perpetrators. That was probably how she had been greeting, the woman, because of the fucking victims, she was a victim, and that's who it was happening to, the fucking victims. He wanted to go home, right now, he wanted fucking out of it, right fucking out of it right fucking now it was a free country and he wanted to get away home for his fucking tea. He glanced along at her, to see what she was doing. She was still holding the carton of coffee, engrossed in the picture. The old dear as well. It was just him. He was the only one that couldnt concentrate. That was that nowadays, how he never seemed able to concentrate, it never fucking seemed to work any more, you couldnt blank it out. He kicked his coffee over. It was a mistake. But he was glad he had done it. He wished they had all fucking seen; it would sort them out, wondering how come he had done it, if it was meant; he got up off the chair and edged his way along to the end of the row, watching he didnt bump into her as he went; she never so much as glanced at him, then the old dear moving her bags in to let him pass, giving him a look as he went, fuck her, even if he stood on one of them with eggs in it, bastard, he just felt so fucking bad, so fucking bad.

(JAMES KELMAN)

CANNIBAL CRACKERS IN AMAZONAS

The fat man sits with his family grouped around him in the entrance to the shop. They are watching a western on TV. Five weeks ago in Puerto Ayacucho there was no television. Now, 7 December 1978, you can look over a set in one of the stores that sell plastic flowers and tinned food and maybe become the first TV family in the jungle.

First TV family in the jungle is not a bad thing to be when you're surrounded by Makiritare or Piaroa Indians living in shacks with newsprint wallpaper and bunches of bananas to sell. Puerto Ayacucho is what they call in guidebooks a 'gateway' town, not that you can find any guidebooks making a big feature of Puerto Ayacucho. You fly in from Caracas if you plan to vanish into the Amazonas jungle or, conversely, the Orinoco river brings you out of the jungle if you have set your heart and mind on the modern world.

The first thing that will strike you if you are Indian is not the sweet biscuits and tinned fruit. After all, you can buy those from the missionaries once you've worked for some cash. It's the television. *Gunsmoke, Wagon Train, Rawhide.* What does it all mean if you've lived your life in the Venezuelan jungle, eating howler monkey, fruit or giant spiders?

After dark we sit and drink cold beer. Salsa is playing in the *cantiña* disco with the red lights so low you might as well be asleep in a hammock by the Orinoco dreaming of vampire bats and crocodiles. Nature is bloody in tooth and claw here. The salsa fights it out to the death with the cinema soundtrack next door. Main feature tonight is *Soylent Green.* For five weeks we've lived on wooden boats, been bitten by ants, bugs, flies and mosquitoes, seen crocodiles speared, birds shot and fish poisoned and have heard no news of media sensations. I dislike Charlton Heston but this night he'll do.

Soylent Green has been called the first 'junk yard futurism' film. Based on Harry Harrison's novel *Make Room! Make Room!*, it tells the story of Manhattan in the near future. Too many people and everything has run out. The poor live on the streets and the privileged live in guarded penthouses. Never mind the near future, you

'Super Cinema', drawing by Edward Burra, c. 1954

151

might think. Let's talk about Caracas highrises and hillside *barrios*. Let's talk about the Caracas rubbish dump with the black vultures, the burnt-out trucks and the tiny shacks built on mountains of paper and shit. Let's talk about New York City.

Never mind. This is cinema, as they say. Not quite the Holloway Odeon, however. Puerto Ayacucho picture palace has the relaxed air of a street market. There are dogs in the aisles between the broken-down seats, sleeping children and booming salsa from the disco. The audience is mostly Indian. Confused, one might guess, since the hum from the loudspeaker system obscures the soundtrack and subtitles are made mysterious by a fungal print quality. Each reel change is lengthy and re-entry into the narrative is haphazard at best.

The nub of the film is soylent green itself. In the future, the hungry are being fed on dead people. These human biscuits, contemptuously called 'idiotic cannibal crackers' by Harry Harrison, are highly desirable items for the turn of the century New Yorker. 'Dreams very confused,' I wrote in my diary the next morning.

Eleven days before *Soylent Green* and four hundred or so miles into the jungle as the river runs we were guests of the Wabutawi-teri, a village of Yąnomamö Indians living on the edge of the Ocamo, a river which strikes northwards from the Orinoco in the direction of the Serra Parima, Brazil. The Yąnomamö practise (if that is the right word) what is known as endo-cannibalism. Occasionally they will mix the ashes of the dead with boiled plantain soup. After dusk we are allowed to watch this ceremony, standing quietly in the dark perimeter of the hut as the container of soup was passed from one naked silhouetted figure to the next. The atmosphere was very moving and dignified. It was tempting to try to record the weird sound of restrained sobbing but this would have been insensitive and impolite, not to say dangerous. The Yąnomamö are not known as 'the fierce people' for nothing.

It goes without saying that human bone soup and cannibal crackers can become fused in the imagination. Perhaps it takes five weeks in the South American jungle to fully appreciate the combined effects of the cinema and

Yąnomamö shaman drawing out the spirit (photo: Odile Laperche, 1978)

film (as opposed to a video in the living room). Some years later I spent an afternoon in the Holloway Odeon Screen 3 watching a *Mad Max* matinee. In the interval between *Mad Max 1* and *2* one of the five people in the audience totters to his feet. By the look of it he's a teenage solvent addict and junk yard futurism aficionado. He stands bathed in the sickly yellow light emanating from the curtains and sings, a capella and in its entirety, Elvis Presley's 'Love Me Tender'.

'Love me tender, love me true, all my dreams fulfil,' he sings. He returns to his seat in a silence that is easily as bad as sitting in chewing gum. The curtains part and *Mad Max 2* begins its tale of the apocalypse.

(DAVID TOOP)

In summer the cinema was outdoors and you sat in rows of deckchairs. The game was to crawl along the aisle and gently dislodge the supports of the deckchairs so that their occupants suddenly fell flat on their backs, shrieking loudly.

(DEIRDRE CLARK)

OASIS

The frost glinted on the fields in the early morning sunshine as the train from Cork pulled into Mallow. A fine day in prospect. Change here for Dublin. Whoever designed Mallow station built the platforms too low or the railway engineers built the trains too high, because there's a five foot drop from the open doors, to each of which a set of steps is wheeled by station staff so that passengers can alight. Everyone seems to know one another and the soft, lilting brogues of West Cork fill the carriages, to be replaced two hours later by the nasal Dublin twang as the train arrives at bustling Heuston station. Across the capital to Connolly station for the Belfast connection. The line runs along the east coast, past marshes, harbours and beaches where children are paddling with frisking dogs. At Dundalk the train stops and we all get off. The IRA have blown up the railway line ahead and we decant into a bus to take us across the border to Poyntzpass where another train awaits. A few miles up the road the bus is stopped at a road block manned by armed soldiers with painted faces. A huge car bomb has gone off without warning in the nearby seaside town of Warrenpoint. One young woman killed, thirty injured. The bus is diverted over the mountains. The roads become lanes, ever narrower until the hedges scrape the sides of the bus which halts periodically when cattle, sheep or goats block the path. It's blistering hot on board and if the rusty air-conditioning vents ever worked they don't now. I try to open the yellow perspex sunroof but it's stuck. A bigger man tries without any more success. Eventually a huge man gets out of his seat, braces himself like a weightlifter and gives an almighty heave. The perspex panel breaks out of its frame and flies away. Everyone laughs and claps as fresh mountain air rushes in. The bus journey has become a surprise scenic coach trip. Not a cloud in the sky, you can see for fifty miles. From the mountain top the views are spectacular and the bus driver, entering into the spirit, points out distant landmarks. In the middle of nowhere we slow down to inspect the Grave of the Long Woman by the roadside.

At Poyntzpass we board the waiting train. Here they use wooden blocks instead of steps. At last there's a buffet car and the train speeds non-stop through Portadown, Lurgan, Lisburn, then the Belfast suburbs, every wall plastered with sectarian graffiti and murals. Clipped, abrasive Belfast accents ring out in the Central Station. The evening sun is setting over the city hall, on the front of which a huge banner proclaims Ulster Says No.

The car cruises through the city centre, past fortified police stations and barracks side by side with pizza parlours, cocktail bars and the Cambridge Diet Counselling Centre. We stop at traffic lights behind an army Landrover, in the back of which sit two soldiers with rifles at the ready. Another soldier in camouflaged battledress stands in the doorway of the Take Six designer boutique, his rifle held in front of his chest. The lights change and we turn into the Newtonards Road and out through Protestant East Belfast. Terraced houses give way to semi-detached, then bigger detached houses with spacious gardens, until, at the end of its mile-long approach road the grandiose palace of Stormont looms into view, as massively overbearing as anything built by Albert Speer. After Stormont the houses get fewer until we reach the village of Comber, a model of suburban order built around a war memorial. It was the

Comber Letter which in the seventeenth century fuelled the Protestant settlers' fears of impending massacre and led to the siege of Derry and the Apprentice Boys whose defiance of King James has been commemorated every year since.

Out past Comber farmland takes over, with only isolated buildings. It's dusk, quiet and still except for the kaas of rooks returning to the rookery. In the half light we go up a small sideroad which we turn off at the end of the big hedge, past a mooing cow alongside a small wooden sign saying Cinema Car Park. And here it is, an expanse of immaculately rolled gravel on the far side of which, framed by palm trees beneath a pale moon, is a tiny white stucco cinema with a red neon sign: the Tudor.

The Tudor cinema, County Down, Ireland (photo: John Kindness, 1989)

Inside the foyer is a ticket and ice cream kiosk. Framed on the walls and in display stands are luridly coloured film posters. *Rodan*: 'The most shocking name in 2000 years.' *The Alligator People. The Monster That Challenged The World. The Thing That Couldn't Die*: 'Every woman who stares into its eyes becomes a willing slave. Every man who confronts it becomes a monster.' *Creature from the Black Lagoon. Blood of the Vampire. The Screaming Skull*: 'The tortured ghost who claimed vengeance in a bride's bedroom.' *The Beast from the Haunted Cave*: 'Screaming young girls sucked into a labyrinth of horror by a blood-starved ghoul from hell.'

The fifty-seater auditorium is lined with thick pile carpeting on floor, walls and ceiling. An illuminated zinc exit sign glows above the door. All outside sound is cut off, just the delicate doo-wop harmonies of the Orioles, 'I Only Have Eyes For You' from the hidden speakers alongside the footlights which illuminate the red velvet curtains covering the screen in anticipation of showtime. The abiding magic of going to the pictures.

In the projection box soundproofed with egg boxes is Noel Spence, who runs the cinema and is one half of Gothic Films, which are directed by his brother Roy and then shown in the cinema to local people as shorts before the main features from their collection of 16mm prints of mainstream and low-budget Hollywood movies. This weekend the forthcoming attraction is 'Steven' McQueen in *The Blob*, but tonight the audience of visitors who have journeyed out from Belfast in a convoy of cars are going to watch some of the Spences' own no-budget creations. Starting with *Phase One*, a condensed, five minute spoof of *2001*, full of inventive special effects. Followed by *Brady's Bargain*, a Blarneyvision ghost story atmospherically shot on location at night, of a greed-crazed search for the leprechauns' gold, and the terrible revenge wreaked by the little people. Then the main movie, *The Wishing Stone*, a tragi-comic saga about a mysterious stone which falls from the sky into the midst of a hillbilly community in the southern states of America, but filmed in County Down with hand-built sets and a cast of local thespians, friends of the Spences, whose melodramatic hamming is perfectly suited to the L'il Abner characters. A world of make believe where the spirit of Georges Méliès and Roger Corman persists in a henhouse turned into a picture palace flanked by palm trees in a County Down field, an oasis in the grey, embittered world outside the muffled doors.

(IAN BREAKWELL)

ECLIPSE

The image on the screen in the sudden darkness was of a woman seated in the sunshine, cutting up a fish. It was inexpressibly beautiful. When on second viewing the image came round it was disappointing, as the colours in a fish you have just caught and thrown into the bottom of the boat swiftly fade before your eyes.

(SUE McNAB)

January 1976. 'Tonight at the London Film-Makers Co-op Cinema, a rare screening of David Larcher's extraordinary *Monkey's Birthday*. Be there or be square.' Well, let no one call me square, so on the stroke of six I switched off the typewriter, fixed my makeup and set off from the office for Camden Town, clacking across the courtyard in my high heels to the cinema.

This was the cinema? An icy concrete room in what had previously been a piano factory. Rows of canvas film directors' chairs already filled with regular patrons who were sensibly equipped with rugs, blankets, primus stoves and thermos flasks of hot soup. I seemed to be the only one not wearing baggy dungarees, scarf, woolly hat and mittens.

'How long is the film?'

'Six hours.'

I wrapped my coat around me and huddled in the canvas chair. The film began: it had no conventional plot or dialogue, but instead an ever more complex series of ravishing abstract colours and grainy textured footage of deserts filmed in shimmering heat. Even so it was difficult to suspend disbelief; after two hours my toes were numb and my teeth beginning to chatter. Another hour passed and my limbs were rigid. Onscreen vivid flashing colours alternated with dark shadows, like a light being switched on and off. I started to join in, squinting, opening my eyes wide, then watching with each eye alternately open or closed. But when I closed my left eye all I could see with my right was a black screen with a pinpoint of light in one corner, and after a time I realised that this did not correspond with the film. Either it was an optical illusion or something was badly wrong with my right eye.

Flashing Dracula at high noon

The following day found me at Moorfields Eye Hospital; it wasn't an optical illusion. After the test the consultant sat me down and spoke in those calm, hushed tones which I knew from a thousand movies meant bad news. I must come in for an operation two days later. From this point on it was as if I'd stepped into a melodrama the script of which was known to everybody except me.

I went back to my flat to sort out my clothes and make arrangements. On the side of the washbasin in the bathroom was my landlord's green glass eye; it was a new one and he took it out at night. He had financed his first cartoon film with the compensation after he had been stabbed in the eye in a street fight. I covered the eyeball with a flannel and made some telephone calls to Wales, from where the news spread like bushfire. My mother took her fur coat out of mothballs, preparing to come up to London for a lengthy stay at my bedside, and fixing up bridge parties for the evenings with old friends she hadn't seen for years. My sister's school said prayers for the success of the operation, and in my home village the local women baked Welsh cakes and the retired district nurse booked Meals on Wheels for the weeks of convalescence.

On Sunday morning I checked in at the hospital.

'Religion?'

'Next of kin?'

The questions went on and on as I sat in the middle of the ward by the table stacked with flowers awaiting distribution to the bedsides. I was informed that if I became a registered blind person I was eligible for a discount on a colour television licence, and allowed a black and white one free. The Radio Moorfield disc jockey asked me if I had any request I would like to be played, pointing out that certain records were not allowed, such as 'I Can See Clearly Now', 'What Do You Want to Make Those Eyes at Me For?' and 'Jeepers Creepers, Where'd You Get Those Peepers?' Orders were taken for talking books, but by now I was distracted: in the distance, but coming nearer, I could hear the sound of tapping and high-pitched hymn singing. Through the ward door came a procession of twelve women in dark glasses led by one with a white stick. Each woman had her hand on the shoulder of the one in front, like elephants at a circus, as they shuffled and hopped along singing 'Lead Kindly Light'. The blind leading the blind in a macabre dance: the final scene of *Seventh Seal* come to life.

Sunday solemnity, flowers, hymn-singing processions, it was all a flashback, a scene replayed: the schoolgirl crocodile and the rigid pews in church. Then, as now, the sniggers and giggles bubbled up uncontrollably. Each step they took only made matters worse, and when I too was issued with my dark glasses I was hysterical. Snorting, laughing and crying I was led away to bed and sedated. I turned my head on the pillow and could dimly make out the twelve women seated beside my bed in their dark glasses while on the television screen above an American cop in dark glasses gazed down at them. As the sleeping pills took effect I wondered if the colours of *Monkey's Birthday*, at the moment I had realised about my affliction, would be indelibly preserved within my eyeball when they took it out and put it in a dish like my landlord did with his false one, or would it be this last, ludicrous image of the women and Kojak in shades? Then everything went black.

(FELICITY SPARROW)

ACKNOWLEDGMENTS

'Darby O'Gill and the Little People' by John Carson was first published in *Picture This: Films Chosen by Artists*, ed. Steve Gallagher, Hallwalls Contemporary Arts Center, Buffalo, New York 1987
'Blind Man's Movie Buff' by Harry Fainlight in *Selected Poems*, Turret Books, London, 1986, ed. Ruth Fainlight
'The Pictures' by James Kelman in *Bête Noire*, Hull, Winter 1989
'Time Flies' and 'Double Death' by Petr Král in *Private Screening*, Frisson, London, 1985
'MOMA' by Lynne Tillman in *Paranoids Anonymous Newsletter*, New York, 1977

Gracias to Phil Derbyshire for his translation of Daniel Moyano's Spanish

For their unstinting support the editors would like to thank:
Mark Ainley, David Attoe, Mark Barnsley, Helen Birch, Josie Brown, Elayne Burrows of the British Film Institute, Jonathan Dennis of the New Zealand Film Archive, Peter Finch, Pete Hodgkiss, Una Hurding, Nick Kimberley, Peter Kravitz, Jill McGreal, Chris Mullen, Jim Nelson, Mr Roebook of Odeon Cinemas, Nottingham, Roy Spence, Parminder Vir

Thanks also to:
Di Atkinson, Monika Baker, Paul Buck, Ade Coker, Rosemary Colvin, Jenny Cudworth, Jackie Duigan, David Dunbar, Jochen Gerz, Ron Haselden, Adrian Henri, John Hopper, John Keane, Alexis Lykiard, John Lyle, John Mead, George Melly, Michael Meyer, Melinda Miel, Jeff Nuttall, Anita Phillips, John Phillips, Tom Pickard, Michael Richardson, Su-G, Martin Trippett, Francis Wright

NOTES ON CONTRIBUTORS

ELENA ALEXANDER is a dancer and choreographer from The Bowery, NYC
J F ARANDA, Luis Buñuel's biographer, writes surrealist poetry in Madrid
PETE AYRTON wags the Serpent's Tail
GLEN BAXTER, noted for his hilarious drawings, possesses the complete recordings of Bill Monroe & the Blue Grass Boys
MELISSA BENN writes for *City Limits*

DAVID BRIERS is a freelance writer on art and lives in Cardiff

NANCEE OKU BRIGHT is awaiting the day she can wear false white eyelashes

STEVE BUCKLEY is features editor on *Mediaweek* magazine

ANGUS CALDER wrote one of the best books on WW2, *The People's War*

JENNI CALDER, an authority on Westerns, once shared a podium with Clint Eastwood

KINGSLEY CANHAM manages Norwich's Cinema City

STEVE CAPLIN edits the magazine *The Truth*

ROGER CARDINAL, an expert on *art brut*, recently published a study of painter Paul Nash

J L CARR publishes *Carr's Dictionary of Extra-ordinary English Cricketers*

JOHN CARSON, Irish humorist, named his firstborn 'Frank'

JOHN CHRISTIE is a video and film lighting cameraman

DEIRDRE CLARK works in publishing and loves opera

JEFF CLOVES is a St Albans anarchist who writes songs and poems

BILL COATES takes photographs in the north-east of England

ANDY COLE was a cinema projectionist for many years

LES COLEMAN, a witty artist, has of late been honing his aphorisms

JOHN CONQUEST sold his houseboat and headed for Texas, where he advises the locals on New Country music

KEVIN COYNE, writer and recording artist, lives in Nuremberg

NICK CUDWORTH'S driving piano has propelled many bands including The Over the Hillbillies

DAVID CURTIS knows more about animated films than Walt Disney

DAVID CUTHBERT paints as well as editing M5 Press in Gloucestershire

IVOR CUTLER is a Scottish poet, musician and humorist

SHARON DELL has worked at the New Zealand Film Archive and is now Keeper of the Collections at the Turnbull Library in Wellington

RAYMOND DURGNAT relishes and writes prolifically about cinema

ANTHONY EARNSHAW, artist and writer, once had the laces blown out of his shoes during a gale

FRANKIE EARNSHAW, daughter of Tony, makes videotapes

MAX EASTLEY invents and plays sound sculptures, and was one half of The Promenaders string section

THERESE EIBEN lives in NYC where she spends much of her time in the dark

JANICE EIDUS'S collection of short stories, *Vito Loves Geraldine*, was published by Serpent's Tail in 1989

MIKE EVANS plays in the r'n'b band Left Hand Jive

HARRY FAINLIGHT'S posthumous *Selected Poems* was edited by his sister Ruth

SALAH FAIQ is a poet from the mountains of Iraq

MRS FINCH'S notes are cherished by her poet son Peter

JO FINN is a magazine production manager

JOHN FURNIVAL, using materials from all over the world, built a famous wall in Gloucestershire

ALAN GARNER has been writing his novels, much appreciated by children and intelligent adults, since 4.03 p.m. on Tuesday 4 September 1956

CHRIS GARRATT is fifty percent of the Biff cartoon team

RON GEESIN, sound architect, even miked his family's lavatory seat

TERRY GENIN is an aficionado of horror films

ANDREW GRAVES was locked in his bedroom by burglars who methodically looted the rest of his house

SUZANNAH HALL is a photographer in Maine, USA

MAGGI HAMBLING paints in her studio next door to Giovanna Cooper

CHRISTINE HAMMOND is an educational adviser

MICK HANNIGAN is the director of the Cork Film Festival

MIKE HARDING, singer, comedian and cyclist, broadcasts frequently

SYLVIA HARKINSON researches into drug dependency

RALPH HAWKINS writes poetry

JULIAN HENRIQUES is currently a filmmaker for BBC Television

LIZ HERON, is a writer and translator and spends a lot of time on the Dieppe ferry

JUDITH HIGGINBOTTOM is the film officer of South West Arts

SELIMA HILL is a poet, her most recent collection being *Accumulation of Small Acts of Kindness*

IAN HINCHLIFFE once fished all night from the back of a ferry bound for Ireland

CHARLIE HOLMES is a friend of Les Coleman's

NEIL HORNICK runs Image Diggers Archive

DAVE HUCKER, once a stalwart of the Electric cinema, is now a DJ and 'Tropical Music Consultant'

PATRICK HUGHES, an artist specialising in humour, has written books on paradoxes, puns and oxymoron. His birthmark is said to resemble a scotty dog

ALYSON STONEMAN HUNTER is a painter and etcher from New Zealand

MALCOLM IMRIE is an editor at Verso Books and an expert on the Marquis de Sade

TONY JACKSON is a Tyneside poet

TIMOTHY EMLYN JONES is a painter and teacher in the West Midlands

NICOLE WARD JOUVE, the biographer of Baudelaire and Colette, wrote a study of 'The Yorkshire Ripper'

NELLY KAPLAN is best known for her film *Dirty Mary* (*La fiancée du pirate*), less known for her erotic novels, written under the pseudonym 'Belen'

JAMES KELMAN, the Glaswegian 'dirty realist', published *A Disaffection* in 1989 to great acclaim

MICK KIDD is the other half of Biff

JOHN KINDNESS is an artist in Belfast, the Monkey Town Besieged by Dogs

PETER KRAL has written two illuminating books in French about silent comedy

JUDY KRAVIS teaches French literature at Cork University

CHRISTOPHER LAIRD makes television programmes in Trinidad & Tobago

MIKE LEGGETT'S minimal guitar playing has emptied many rooms

GEORGE LITTLEBLACK reviews sports videos

VIEANNE LYLE has a parrot named Abu who breakfasts daily on toast and marmalade

GERRY McCARTHY writes for *In Dublin* magazine

ALF MacGABHAN, a Dubliner, works for British Telecom

DAVID MacLAGAN is a painter, art therapist and translator of Artaud

ALASTAIR MacLENNAN is a performance artist in Belfast

SUE McNAB is an authority on medieval Irish art

MARCEL MARIEN, a survivor of Belgian surrealism, makes very funny objects and has written a scandalous autobiography

MURRAY MARTIN is the eminence grise behind Newcastle's Amber Films

J H MATTHEWS was, until his recent death, the Welsh-American author of many books on surrealism

ROLAND MILLER is a performance artist in Sheffield

LIONEL MISKIN lives, draws and writes in Cyprus

DEBORAH MOGGACH, the novelist, is published by Penguin

LISA MONTAGUE works in an old people's home in the Channel Islands

DANIEL MOYANO, the Argentinian novelist living in exile in Spain, is known to English readers for his *The Devil's Trill*

ARTHUR MOYSE is a life-long anarchist who used to be a London bus driver

JOHN MUCKLE wrote the obituary of Roy Orbison in *The Guardian*

JAMIE MUIR is a very tall television producer

DENIS NORDEN, aficionado of the out-take, was once the UK's youngest cinema manager

P P O'LEARY, a potter, divides his time between Donegal and Bolton

MICHAEL O'PRAY, co-director of the Film & Video Umbrella, last year edited the book *Andy Warhol: Film Factory*

DEBORAH ORR is deputy editor of *City Limits*

DES O'SULLIVAN reports the news for *The Cork Examiner*

CHARLES PELTZ, a conveyancer, has a monstrous collection of books on Eros and Thanatos

HILARY PHILLIPS still chuckles every time she climbs into the bath

CHRIS PROCTOR, for many years a trades union negotiator, now lives and writes in France

KATE PULLINGER recently published her first novel, *When the Monster Dies*

DONNA RAE designed stage sets in America before moving to Glasgow to sculpt

TOM RAWORTH'S book of selected poems, *Tottering State*, has been published by Paladin

PAUL ROBINSON is a photographer in Nottingham

JONATHAN ROSENBAUM wrote the seminal moviegoer's autobiography, *Moving Places*

BARBARA SAMUELS is a film director and producer in Montreal

CAROLEE SCHNEEMANN, filmmaker and multi-media artist, kisses cats in NYC

DEREK SMITH is a television producer who lives entirely on fish

T DAN SMITH, Newcastle town planner, has clung to his belief in civic pride through thick and thin

CHERRY SMYTH is editing a book for Virago on the representation of women in cinema

FELICITY SPARROW has the loudest scream in Wales

JO SPENCE'S self-portrait photographs, exploring the themes of sexuality, myth and power, have been widely exhibited

NOEL SPENCE runs the Tudor cinema in County Down with his brother Roy

MARTY ST JAMES plans to collaborate on a series of provincial civic monuments using live elements

ROD STONEMAN is a commissioning editor for Channel Four Television

LYNNE TILLMAN writes, directs films and lives in Manhattan

DAVID TOOP is an author and a musician, the other half of The Promenaders string section

LAWRENCE UPTON ardently supports European monetary union

TOM WAKEFIELD has written autobiography, short stories and, of late, a new novel, *Lot's Wife*

ROGER WAKELING did art therapy with mentally handicapped people for ten years

MONONA WALI is a filmmaker

IAN WALKER takes droll photographs and lives in Newport

ERIC WALLACE is the newsreader for Border Television

JOHN WELSON paints surrealist pictures and collects jazz records

ANNE WILSON collaborates with Marty St James and once ran a very strange hotel with him

MARLENE WINFIELD is a researcher into poverty

ELIZABETH J YOUNG writes feisty book reviews and lives by the
River Thames

HAFIA ZANGANA, from Baghdad, collages and dispenses medicine
to Londoners

PICTURE CREDITS

The National Film Archive, London
The Cinema Theatre Association (David Jones) c/o The Odeon,
Streatham High Road, London SW16
The Anthony Reynolds Gallery, London
The Lefevre Gallery, London
CBS Fox
Palace Pictures
Susan Ormerod
Mike Zwerin